Wood Pallets Projects Collection
82 Plans to Try

Copyright 2016 by the publisher - All rights reserved.

This document is geared towards providing exact and reliable information in regards to the topic and issue covered. The publication is sold with the idea that the publisher is not required to render accounting, officially permitted, or otherwise, qualified services. If advice is necessary, legal or professional, a practiced individual in the profession should be ordered.

From a Declaration of Principles which was accepted and approved equally by a Committee of the American Bar Association and a Committee of Publishers and Associations.

In no way is it legal to reproduce, duplicate, or transmit any part of this document in either electronic means or in printed format. Recording of this publication is strictly prohibited and any storage of this document is not allowed unless with written permission from the publisher. All rights reserved.

The information provided herein is stated to be truthful and consistent, in that any liability, in terms of inattention or otherwise, by any usage or abuse of any policies, processes, or directions contained within is the solitary and utter responsibility of the recipient reader. Under no circumstances will any legal responsibility or blame be held against the publisher for any reparation, damages, or monetary loss due to the information herein, either directly or indirectly.

Respective authors own all copyrights not held by the publisher.

The information herein is offered for informational purposes solely, and is universal as so. The presentation of the information is without contract or any type of guarantee assurance.

The trademarks that are used are without any consent, and the publication of the trademark is without permission or backing by the trademark owner. All trademarks and brands within this book are for clarifying purposes only and are the owned by the owners themselves, not affiliated with this document.

All photos used in this book, including the cover photo were made available under a Attribution 2.0 Generic (CC BY 2.0) and sourced from Flickr.

Table of Contents

Book 1

20 Ways To Use Wood Pallets In Your Garden 8
Introduction 9
Chapter 1 – Garden Furniture with Wooden Pallet 10
    Use 01: Pallet Sofa...10
    Use 02: Shelves for Garden 11
    Use 03: DIY Garden Chair 13
    Use 04: DIY Coffee Table 14
    Use 05: Pallet Stool for Garden..15
Chapter 2 – Garden Decorations with Pallet 18
    Use 06: DIY Pallet Fence 18
    Use 07: DIY Pallet Box...19
    Use 08: Magnetic Rack for Fertilizers and Seeds..21
    Use 09: Pallet Rack 21
    Use 10: Pallet Posts 23
Chapter 3 – Storage Bin and Garden Beds..25
    Use 11: Pallet Compost Bin 25
    Use 12: Design Frame for Vegetables 26
    Use 13: Design a Beautiful Bed for Garden 28
    Use 14: Tips to Grow Your Herbal Garden...29
    Use 15: Rack to Keep Your Tools 30
Chapter 4 – DIY Pallet Fences, Walls and Pathway 33
    Use 16: Bird House 33
    Use 17: Pallet Bin for Compost and Plants 34
    Use 18: Pallet Pathway 35
    Use 19: Pallet Playhouse 37

Use 20: Storage Shed for Garden 38

Chapter 5 – Tips to Check if the Wooden Pallet is Usable 41

Tools Required for Pallet Projects 41

Conclusion 43

Book 2

Building with Wood Pallets 44

Fun & Easy Projects for Young and Old 44

Introduction 45

Coffee Mug Rack 50

Deck Chair 53

Shipping Crate Storage Table 56

Minimal Pallet Bed 58

Food Serving Cart on Wheels 61

Pallet Plank Shelf 63

Rustic Drinks Cooler 65

Garden Planter 68

Two Seater Chair 71

Conclusion 73

Book 3

DIY .... Ошибка! Закладка не определена.77

25 Woodworking Projects To Decorate Your Space 74

Introduction 75

Chapter 1 – 15 Incredible Woodworking Projects To Decorate Your Indoors 76

Woodworking Project 01: Make white indoor sofa set: 76

Woodworking Project 02: Make vintage pallet sectional sofa: 77

Woodworking Project 03: Join pallets and hang different things: 79

Woodworking Project 04: Make pallet sofa with some storage: 80

Woodworking Project 05: Project for kitchen: 81

Woodworking Project 06: Make vase and other decoration pieces: 82

Woodworking Project 07: Make indoor pallet swing chair: 84

Woodworking Project 08: Make Pallet pot rack for your kitchen: 85

Woodworking Project 09: Make rusting pencil holders: 86

Woodworking Project 10: Make indoor daybed: 87

Woodworking Project 11: Make indoor coffee table: 88

Woodworking Project 12: Make pallet sectional sofa and matching table for indoor: 90

Woodworking Project 13: Make book shelves: 91

Woodworking Project 14: Make pallet teen girl bed: 92

Woodworking Project 15: Make pallet wall panel: 93

Chapter 2 – 10 Woodworking Projects To Decorate Your Outdoor Space 95

Woodworking Project 01: Make outdoor pallet table: 95

Woodworking Project 02: Outdoor pallet sitting plan: 96

Woodworking Project 03: Make outdoor pallet fence: 97

Woodworking Project 04: Make beautiful wall garden: 98

Woodworking Project 05: Make comfy daybed for outdoor: 99

Woodworking Project 6: Sectional sofa and moveable table for outdoor: 100

Woodworking Project 7: Make bar with stools for outdoor: 100

Woodworking Project 8: Make pallet bench and gabion table: 101

Woodworking Project 9: Make place for pots: 102

Woodworking Project 10: Make L shaped outdoor sitting plan: 103

Conclusion 105

Book 4

Wood Pallet Projects 106

DIY Projects That are Easy to Make and Sell 106

Introduction 107

Chapter 1 – Pallet Home Accessories... 108

    Project 1 – Wood Pallet Wall clocks 108

    Project 2 – Pallet bookshelf 113

    Project 3 – Pallet Flag 115

Chapter 2 – Wood Pallet Furniture.. 117

    Project 1 – Coffee Table... 117

    Project 2 – Outdoor Garden/Patio furniture 120

Chapter 3 – Wooden Pallet Art and Décor 125

    Project 1 – Wall cover up.. 125

    Project 2 – Wine Rack 126

    Project 3 – Ornamental Christmas tree 127

    Project 4 – Wooden Pallet Wall Art... 128

    Project 5 – Lamp base... 131

Chapter 4 – DIY Garden Racks and Décor from Wood Pallets........................... 133

    Project 1 – Pot Rack... 133

    Project 2 – Vertical Herb Garden.. 135

    Project 3 – Garden Path... 138

Conclusion 142

<u>Book 5</u>

Wood Pallet Projects for Beginners... 144

15 DIY Household Hacks to Reuse Wood Pallets and Decorate Your Space

Introduction 145

Chapter 1 - Wood Pallet Wall..147

Chapter 2 - Wine Rack...149

Chapter 3 - Planter...151

Chapter 4 - Decorative Tray...153

Chapter 5 - Electronics Shelf 155

Chapter 6 - Bike Rack..157

Chapter 7 - Herb Trough..158

Chapter 8 - Spice Rack..159

Chapter 9 - Compost Bin 161

Chapter 10 - Desktop Planter 163

20 Ways To Use Wood Pallets In Your Garden

Introduction

Wood pallets are popular for outdoor and home projects because these are cheap and easily available for your projects. You can design different items for home and outdoor uses. In your garden, you will need different items, such as table and sofa for sitting arrangements. You should have a separate place to store your garden tools and other essential items. With the help of pallet, you can design different projects from beds, coffee tables, window boxes, comfortable rockers, shoe cabinets and various other projects.

Furniture designed with wood pallets is perfect for your balcony, patio, garden area, etc. You will need raised beds in the garden for your plants and compost bins. With the help of pallet, you can design a birdhouse, storage shed, chairs, practical benches and lots of other things. The pallet is an economical choice for you because it is easily available in your backyard or you can even buy from the market at low rates. With the help of a swing and different racks, you can increase beauty and storage area of your garden area.

If you want to arrange furniture for your garden within your budget, you can select pallets to complete your work. Pallet pet bed, outdoor shower and playhouse for your children can be designed with the help of pallet wood. You should be careful while purchasing pallet wood and try to get wood pallets in good condition. There are a few projects that will help you to design different types of furniture for your garden. You can design a nice rocker, chair, swing and other accessories for your personal garden. A garden bench will offer additional sitting arrangement.

This book is designed for your help so that you can learn 20 beautiful uses of wood pallets that will help you to design your own furniture. These DIY projects are really good for you to design your own pallet furniture.

Chapter 1 – Garden Furniture with Wooden Pallet

If you want patio or garden furniture, you can use wood pallets to design sofa, table, chair and other items:

Use 01: Pallet Sofa
You can design a sofa with the pallet to decorate your patio and garden area. There are a few tips to design pallet sofa:

Collect Your Pallet

The average size of pallet will be 9 and you should select the best quality pallets to design sofa. You can find some cool wood burned or stamped wood. It is important to check a few extra details.

Cut Pallets

You have to cut these pallets at 27.5 inches wide to mix and match them easily. You can cut straight across the slats and remove a few inches on the side 2 by 4. You can reuse 2 by 4 by sliding it into the gap and reattach with the help of nails. The overall length can be 78" x 78".

Create Cushions

You have to hide front 2 by 4 gap of the pallet with cushions and mattresses. You can use a few mattresses to create your own cushion because the foam can be expensive and you can cut an old mattress to make cushions.

Secure Backs

You can use a few screws to overlap pallets and screw them along the seam. It will be good to use 2-inch screws. You can decorate your patio and use in parties for extra sitting arrangements.

Use 02: Shelves for Garden
- Sandpaper
- Drill, Level, and Hammer
- 2 wood pallets
- Wood screws
- Wood, 2 by 4 inches
- Saw and Nails
- Paint and Paintbrush
- Wall anchors

Instructions:

- In the first step, you have to sand the surface of the wood to get smooth surface pallets. You can use the underside of each pallet.

- Wood screws and drills will be used to attach the pallets to each other. Keep one pallet on the top of the each pallet in the same direction. The undersides will grasp the shelves.

- Gauge the interior of the top pallet for width and cut the wood in the size of 2 by 4 inches. Insert this wood in the horizontal direction into the pallet and keep it 6 to 8 inches from the top of the wood. Check the level of the wood to make sure it is even before keeping it on the top of the wood. Secure the shelf with the use of hammer and nails. Repeat the same process for every shelf.

- You can paint your shelves or leave them unfinished to get a rustic look. With the help of wall studs or anchors, you can fix the shelving unit into the wall.

Use 03: DIY Garden Chair

- Miter saw

- Flat bar

- 2 Wooden pallets

- Nail puller

- Box, stainless steel screws

- Measurement tape

- Screw gun

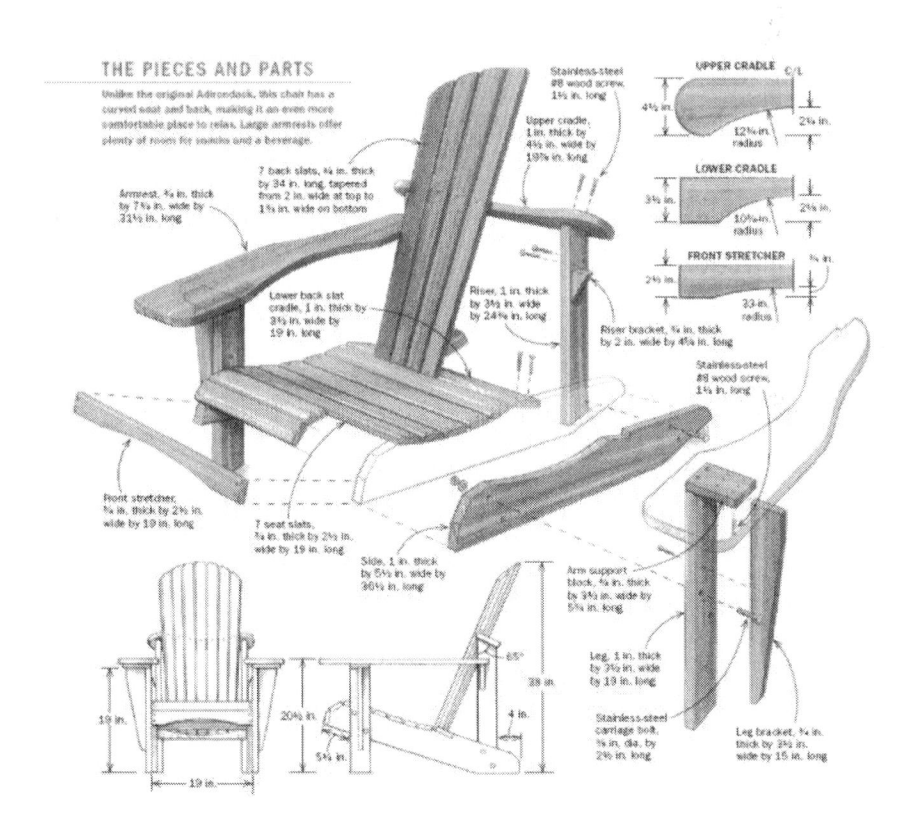

Directions:

- Take a wooden pallet and keep it flat on the work surface with the peak surface facing up. The flat bar will slide under the first two boards at one end of the pallet and snoop them carefully.

- Pull out the nails of every pallet board with the help of nail puller. Clean the pallets by removing any drifted nails and set the boards on one side. Repeat this process and remove the nails from each board and cut the pallet boards for the back of the chair, legs and arms.

- Take two boards and measure the 12-inch surface with the help of measure tape and pencil. Use miter saw and cut to the length of the front leg.

- Place the end, conflicting the detached boards, on the seat assembly pallet and lift it in an upward direction. Keep one front leg on each side at the elevated end and drive four wood screws with equal space through the leg into the exterior of the pallet with the use of screw gun.

- Put the second pallet level on the surface while keeping the top surface in an upward direction. Remove half board from one end of the pallet and clean it by pulling the nails out with the help of nail puller. This pallet will help you to assemble seat and ends with the removal of boards for back legs.

- Insert the pallet designed for a back seat with the back leg down through the fourth board. Bring down the back legs on the work surface and used four screws to fasten the seat. You can use a screw gun to fix the each joint of the chair.

Use 04: DIY Coffee Table
- Drill

- Hot glue gun

- Paint or stain

- Chest or suitcase

- Staple gun

- Measuring tape
- Legs and Storage containers
- Top plate hardware
- Velvet or fabric
- Wallpaper
- Cording or trim
- Wooden dividers

Directions:

Sand the pallet woods and then paint them to complement the colors of your chest. Carefully examine the chest and remove any torn fabric to give a neat look to your coffee table storage.

Measure the legs and then prepare all four legs to secure them at a right place. You can use a machine gun to fix nails and use wooden dividers to make small compartments. It will be good to decorate your wooden dividers with wallpaper.

Use 05: Pallet Stool for Garden
- 4 pieces of wood to make the legs of the stool (3 inches thick)

- Drill and wood glue
- 4 inch thick wood for seat
- Chisel
- 4 large screws
- Varnish
- Padding and upholstery

Directions:

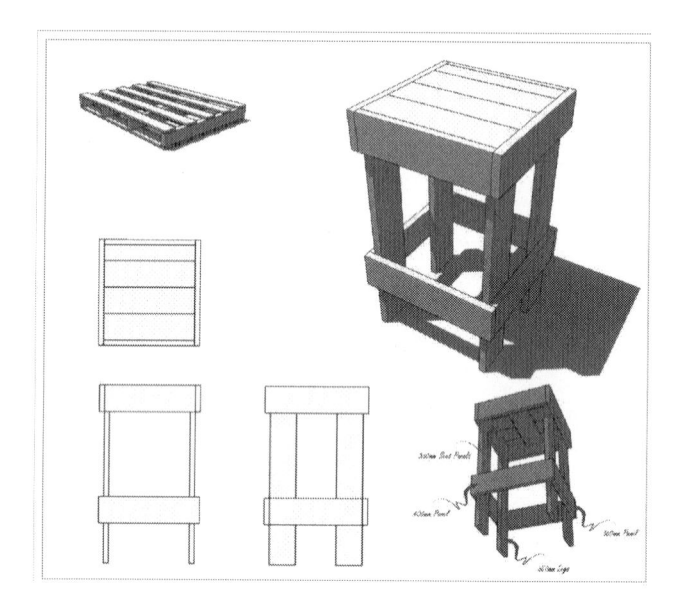

Measure the stool as per your needs and then select pallet wood to make the stool. Cut into different pieces of the wood to make legs and seat. The seat can be round or square.

Drill holes in the seat to fix legs in the four corners, you need to insert screws into each of the four corners on the bar stool. Cut down the legs to determine the height of your stool and try to keep these pieces 3 inches thick. Make sure to keep the size of all four legs same.

You can use wood glue in the holes of the seat around the screw head and carefully insert the legs into the hole. Screw them until you get resistance and make sure to keep it tight. Clean the excessive glue and let the stool dry.

Chapter 2 – Garden Decorations with Pallet

There are a few decorations that can be designed with pallets and these can increase the beauty of your garden:

Use 06: DIY Pallet Fence
- Wooden pallets
- Steel T-posts
- Sledgehammer
- 2 x 4 blocks, 8 inches in length
- Drill/driver
- 3/16-inch drill tad
- 1/4-inch rivets
- Hinges

Directions:

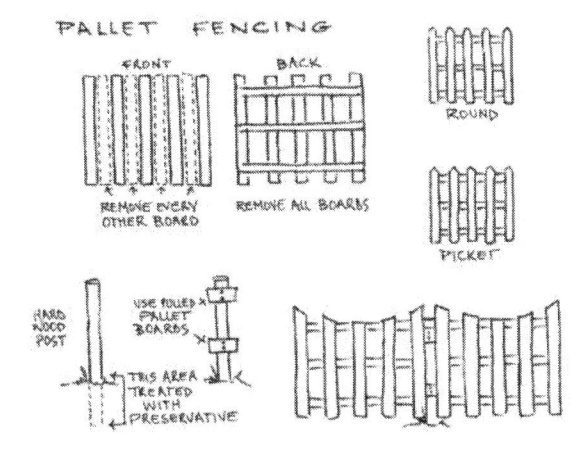

It is really simple, just measure the pallet woods and then cut the vertical pallet boards. Place each perpendicular in a line and use long deck screws and thicker frame wood to stick them together. The size of the post will be based on your own requirements.

Use 07: DIY Pallet Box

- Pencil
- Pallet Wood
- White paper
- Measuring tape
- Hammer
- Saw
- Paint or stain for wood
- Nails
- Paint brush

Directions:

Select a durable pallet and break it by removing nails with the claw of a hammer. You can keep these nails aside and cut the wood to have 14 straight plans with 14.5 inches length. You have to sand every piece to remove rough surfaces.

Set four planks of 14.5 inches and nail them together. This will help you to make one side of the wall of a planter box. Replicate this process with four more planks of 14.5 inches to create a 2nd side wall. You have to create vertical planks for all walls.

Now, you will alight three planks, side by side and use nails to attach them together to make sides of walls. This will make the front wall with vertical planks and replicate this process to make back wall and nails all walls to the front and back walls.

You have to make the base of two runners by cutting two planks equal to your longest wall. This length will be based on the width of your planks. Cut equal short pieces to use as feet and you will need four pieces. Use nails to attach the feet to the underside of all runners.

You have to measure a plank to create a base and cover the open base area of the four walls. They will be placed adjacent to each other. Now nail the two runners on the opposite sides and create a base for measuring planks to the underneath of your base.

Keep the walls of this box on the base and nail it along the bottom of the walls into the base. Place the finished box at the desired place in your garden or yard after filling with desired products.

Use 08: Magnetic Rack for Fertilizers and Seeds

You can use small to large mason jars to secure seeds and chemicals. It is easy to mount a sheet of stainless steel to any wall of your garden. Now use gluing magnets to top canning lids and secure your jars on the wall. It will be good to use a paper chit to label each jar.

Use 09: Pallet Rack
- 4-by-4 posts of 96-inch, 6 pieces

21

- 2-by-6 lumber of 96 inches, 8 pieces

- Square frame

- 4-penny nails (box nails)

- Hammer

- 40 hangers (joist) for lumber

- 16-penny nails

- 2-by-6 lumber of 30 inches, 8 pieces

- 2-by-6 lumber of 27-inch, 20 pieces

Directions

You should arrange a work table and keep six 4 by 4 posts on it. Now measure from one end of the lumber to another end and mark at the point of 30, 60 and 90 inches.

Now put the eight lumber pieces of 2 by 2 on the table and keep them parallel to each other and make sure that they are touching long edges. Measure from the left end and mark each 16 inches. Now keep the frame square on this mark and draw a line transversely the width of your lumber.

Select a mid point on marks for joist hangers and secure them in the 96-inch lumber with the help of 4-penny nails. Make sure to drive all the nails at a slope to avoid their protruding from the other sides of your lumber. Now split two 4-by-4 posts almost 96 inches distant and adjust the third one in the middle.

It is time to take one of 2-by-6 eight pieces lumber to keep on the bottom of the 96-inch posts while keeping the face joist hangers in the downward direction. You can use 16-penny nails to secure them and one post should be there at the end of 2-by-6 lumber and one in the middle. You can replicate this procedure with the remaining posts and lumber as well.

Now you have to turn one of the assemblies above to keep the face of hangers up. It is time to secure the 30-inch lumber to the both ends of 96-inch lumber with 16-penny nails.

Stand the assembly upright to keep the 96-inch pieces with hangers, so that this can meet 30-inch lumber and secure them with 16-inch penny nails.

You can keep one of the 27-inch lumber in every joist hanger and secure them with 4-penny nails.

Use 10: Pallet Posts

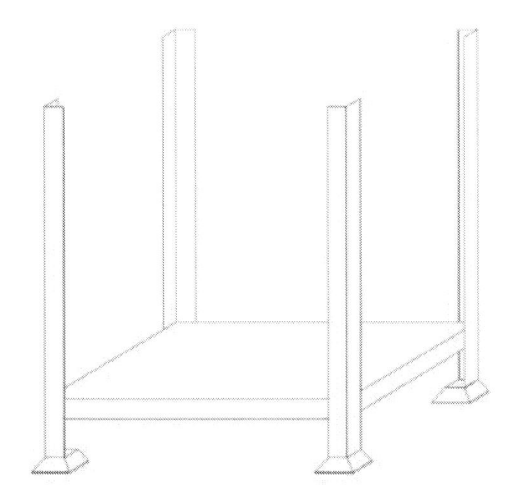

- Steel T-posts
- Sledgehammer
- 2 x 4 blocks, 8 inches in length
- Drill/driver
- 3/16-inch drill tad
- 1/4-inch rivets
- Hinges

Directions:

It is really simple, just measure the pallet woods and then cut the vertical pallet boards. Place each perpendicular in a line and use long deck screws and thicker frame wood to stick them together. The size of the post will be based on your own requirements.

Chapter 3 – Storage Bin and Garden Beds

You can design a few storage bins and garden beds with the help of pallet to save space and money:

Use 11: Pallet Compost Bin
- 5 Pallets
- 6 stakes of 18-inch, 1 x 1
- Mallet
- 2 stakes of 72-inch, 2 x 2
- Staple Gun
- Garden Netting
- Wire Ties, 1 bag
- Scissors

Directions:

Lay out three pallets vertical to make a three-sided box in a place that you want to select for your compost bin.

Now glide a wire tie via the corner at the middle, top and bottom of the pallets to tie them together. Now put a wire tightly and slide stacks all through the middle of the side pallets of the compost bin. Place them at the front edge of the side and force the stakes into the floor. They will be flushed with the top boundaries of the side pallets.

Use 12: Design Frame for Vegetables
- 5 Pallets
- 6 stakes of 18-inch, 1 x 1
- Mallet
- 2 stakes of 72-inch, 2 x 2
- Staple Gun
- Garden Netting
- Wire Ties, 1 bag

- Scissors

Directions:

Select a place in the garden for vegetables, such as pumpkin or squash to grow in A-frame trellis. Keep two boards across the plot to make a 45-degree angle with two pallets and make an A-frame.

Glide wire ties all through the pallets at the top junction and space should be 6 inches along the joints. Tie them tightly.

Now drive 3, 1 x 1 stakes of 18 inches through the bottom of every pallet of the A-frame and secure the frame in its place. Keep one on every end and another in the middle. Roll the garden net to the frame and staple it for security. Clip extra netting and it will help vegetables to grow on the trellis.

Use 13: Design a Beautiful Bed for Garden

- Packing Pallets
- Fertilizer
- Garden Loam
- Organic Compost

Directions:

Set pallets on the smooth ground, but the location should have plenty of sunlight for 6 to 8 hours and air movement. A smooth and level surface will keep the pallets secure and you can raise gardens to quickly use moisture and retain moisture and nutrients of the soil.

Now fill the pallets with soil and pack the soil between slates and on the top. You should have 2 to 3 inches of soil mix over the top of pallets. Soil will be layered in all pallets and the fertilizer can be slowly released into the soil in the rows between the boards. These will be planting rows 4 inches of soil on the top.

It will be good to raise small plants in this garden to avoid overcrowding of roots. These are good for broccoli, cauliflower, cabbage, collards and lettuce.

Use 14: Tips to Grow Your Herbal Garden
- Wall adhesive
- Tapcon screws
- Wooden pallet
- Hose clamps
- Mason jars
- Soil
- Cable Staples
- Charcoal
- Stones
- Plants

Directions:

Use a wood that will serve as a base for the wall and place hose clamps on this wooden board. You can measure the place on a wooden board to find out the capacity of glass jars on the wooden board. If you want to grow herbs, these should be located close to your window. You can grow sage, rosemary, and similar herbs.

After securing the boards in its place, you can use adhesive to secure the board and use tap con screw to make it secure in its place. Now you will measure the center to fix the hose clamps and secure them in their right place.

Pour stones in the bottom of mason jars and make sure these should be free from drainage. After stones, you can add charcoal to balance the pH of soil and avoid growth of bacteria in soil. Now add soil and plants in every jar and secure them with the hose clamps.

Use 15: Rack to Keep Your Tools

- 1 pallet
- Staples
- 4' x 4' chicken wire
- 6 wire coat hangers
- Durable chain
- 2 1/4 x 4" clasp hook bolts and nuts
- 4 washers with bolts
- S-shaped hooks
- Circular Saw and Hammer

- Nail Puller and Nails

- Drill and head screwdriver

- Staple gun and wire cutters

- Tape to Measure

Directions:

Cut the pallets and remove the middle bar of the pallet. Carefully split the wood and measure the split pieces. You should use a staple gun to staple the chicken wire in a particular place. Staple the chicken wire to the wooden bar.

Cut the additional wire with the help of a wire cutter and bend the remaining wire to make the sharp corners smooth. Take the wooden bars and fix the chicken wire with the help of screws and use a nail gun to fix the wood pallets.

Fix the chain along the length and hang the rack at about a 45-degree angle with hook bolts on the wall. Your pot rack is ready and now you can use bolts to fix the rack at a point where you can access it and create additional support.

You can place S-hooks on the hanger wire so that you can hang pots and pans on the hooks. Keep it in mind that these hooks can carry a lightweight item, but you can get the benefits of additional storage.

Chapter 4 – DIY Pallet Fences, Walls and Pathway

There are a few projects that can be followed to surround your garden with walls, fences and pathways:

Use 16: Bird House

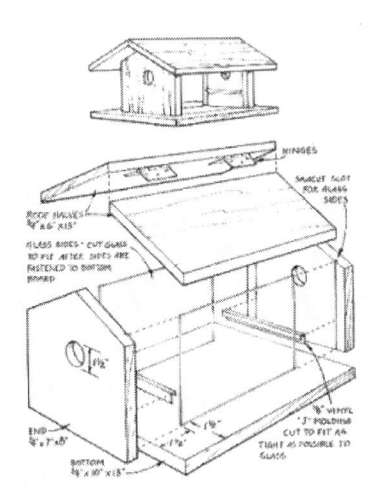

If you want to design a birdhouse, you can get the advantage of pallet wood. You can follow the given plans and blueprint to design your bird house. You have to create a door at the bottom edge of the front piece, but mark it with a pencil. You can cut out the rectangle or round door.

Line up the back panel and the panels on both the sides and fix with nail and hammer along the length of the panels. Now secure the front panel with hammering electrified nails.

It is time to set the wooden frame on the top of the bottom piece and fix it with two to three nails on each corner. Keep a flat panel in its place with hammer and nails and keep it secure. Add adhesive constructions and let the pet house dry.

Use 17: Pallet Bin for Compost and Plants

- 8-foot pieces of 1 x 4 pine, 2 boards
- 10-foot pieces of 1 x 2 pine, 2 boards
- 10-foot piece of 2 x 2 pine, 1 board
- Measuring tape and Clamp
- Safety goggles
- Circular saw
- 1 box of about 1 1/4-inch screws
- Drill and 7/16 drill bit

Directions:

Cut all the wooden pieces with the help of a circular saw, such as you need 4 pieces of 24-inch of 1 x 4, 4 pieces of 22 inches, 4 pieces of 2 x 2 at 30 inches. You will also cut 4 pieces of 1 x 2 at 24 inches and 6 pieces of 25 inches.

You need to build four walls, two walls will be built by 22-inch piece of 1 x 4 and two walls can be designed with 24-inch one x four pieces. You will make square walls build the corners. Fasten them together and assemble the top and bottom area.

Cut the sections for inner rack and drill a screw in each rack to fix it. Finish off the bottom part and prepare the top part in the same way. You can add sealant or paint to protect the rack.

Use 18: Pallet Pathway
- Measuring tape
- Screwdriver
- Pencil
- Wood screws

- Saber saw

Directions:

In the first step, you will measure the width of your path to count the number of pallets required to design it. These are available in different sizes so you should consider the size of your bed and you will need more than one pallet.

You should gauge the width of pallets and keep one pallet flat (upside-down) on the floor. You can make a pencil mark to the place where you want to cut it short.

Cut the pallet wood with the help of a saber saw and remove excessive sections of the pallet.

Now, turn full and cut pallets (upside-down) and line them with each other to make a full-width headboard. Remove excessive board and use it to extend the junction point of two pallets. It is time to drive wood screws into the board to attach all sections.

You can keep this pallet way on the path.

Use 19: Pallet Playhouse

- 1 sheet 1/2-inch pallet wood, 8 feet x 4 feet
- Circular saw and Hammer
- Tape measure
- Straight edge
- 2-inch galvanized nails
- Pencil
- Construction adhesive

Directions:

Cut the pieces of pallet wood boards for the following measurements:

- 21 x 34 inches for bottom
- 27 x 39 inches for top
- 23 x 24 inches for back
- 23 x 24 inches for front

- 24 x 34 inches for side

- 24 x 34 inches for another side

You have to create a door at the bottom edge of the front piece, but mark it with a pencil. You can cut out the rectangle or round door.

Line up the back panel and the panels on both the sides and fix with nail and hammer along the length of the panels. Now secure the front panel with hammering electrified nails.

It is time to set the wooden frame on the top of the bottom piece and fix it with two to three nails on each corner. Keep a flat panel in its place with hammer and nails and keep it secure. Add adhesive constructions and let the pet house dry.

Use 20: Storage Shed for Garden

- Tape Measure

- 1 board of 24 feet, 2 x 4 inch

- Flour
- Jig saw
- Rubber mallet
- 6 Reber of 4 foot
- Hammer
- 3 lengths of 14 PVC pipe, ¾ inch and 12 feet long
- Polyethylene 12 x 2 feet plastic
- Nails
- Fencing staples
- Wire

Directions:

Gauge the footprint of your transferable garage. You have to mark this particular area with flour. The garage should be 6' long and 4' wide.

You can hammer the supports of Rebar halfway into the floor at each corner of the garage along with the rubber mallet. Now hammer the leftover supports into the ground halfway on every side of the shed.

Curve every piece of the PVC to make a U-shape and keep arm of every U at the end of Rebar support gluing out of the floor.

Now drape a wire all the way around the bend of the first segment of PVC pipe. Now, loosely run a wire to the 2nd segment of pipe and drape it. You can expand the wire to the last segment of pipe and drape it loosely. You can create a ridge post that will be good to bear the weight of snow.

Now cut the board into two pieces of 6-foot and one piece of 4-foot. You need additional wood to make an open square. You can keep this square at the bottom of the garage frame outer surface of the Rebar and leave a single side open.

It is time to pull the polyethylene shell at the peak of the garage border to keep one side flush to the façade of the garage. You can nail it down with the fencing tacks. It is time to leave a back lynching loose so that the wind can escape out from the front to the back and the rain will not come as well.

Chapter 5 – Tips to Check if the Wooden Pallet is Usable

Wooden pallets are really helpful to design economic furniture for your house. If you are using wooden pallets found in your backyard, then there is no harm in their use, but if you are purchasing pallets from the market, then it is important to consider some important points:

Make sure your selected pallets are not treated with methyl bromide, and in several countries, these are hard to find. The pallets treated with methyl bromide are banned in New Zealand, Europe, Canada and Australia. Methyl bromide is not good for your health because this dangerous chemical can affect both people and the environment. You should select pallets that are untreated or treated with heat instead of poison.

If the pallet is made for export, then it is a heat treated pallet and it is good for your use. The pallets are treated with heat at 56°C for softwood and 60°C for hardwood to kill pests.

Tools Required for Pallet Projects
If you want to successfully complete different pallet projects, then it is important to have the following tools:

- Pallet Wood
- Nail Gun
- Drill to drill the nails
- Wood glue to use nail gun
- Electric Sander for wood
- Electric Saw to cut the Wood
- Thick gloves (Cut Proof)

- Goggles

- Hat to cover your head

There are two types of pallets, one is for once use and the second pallets are for multiple uses. The cheap softwood pallets are for one-time use only, while the multiple use pallets are designed for the use of hardwood.

Conclusion

In your garden, you will need different items, such as table and sofa for sitting arrangements. You should have a separate place to store your garden tools and other essential items. With the help of pallet, you can design different projects from beds, coffee tables, window boxes, comfortable rockers, shoe cabinets and various other projects. There are a few projects that will help you to design different types of furniture for your garden. You can design a nice rocker, chair, swing and other accessories for your personal garden. A garden bench will offer additional sitting arrangement.

Furniture designed with wood pallets is perfect for your balcony, patio, garden area, etc. You will need raised beds in the garden for your plants and compost bins. With the help of pallet, you can design a birdhouse, storage shed, chairs, practical benches and lots of other things. The pallet is an economical choice for you because it is easily available in your backyard or you can even buy from the market at low rates. With the help of a swing and different racks, you can increase beauty and storage area of your garden area.

Wooden pallets are really helpful to design economic furniture for your house. If you are using wooden pallets found in your backyard, then there is no harm in their use, but if you are purchasing pallets from the market, then it is important to consider some important points. These points are given in this book for your assistance.

Wood Pallets Projects

Introduction

Safety First

This book contains some projects that children might enjoy helping out with. However, adults should always be in charge of the building, especially when power tools are being used.

Why Build with Pallets?

If you're interested in home DIY projects and "upcycling" (that is, using pre-existing items to create new and different items), you have probably already seen lots of wood pallet projects being shared all over the internet.

If you're not totally up-to-date with this new trend, of building things out of old pallets, take a moment to familiarize yourself with the concept. All sorts of goods are transported by ship, plane, and truck. After that, they're generally moved with forklifts and other machines. The wooden pallets are what the goods are loaded on top of, so they will have a stable surface to move around on.

Once these pallets have passed their usefulness, and they are no longer fit to be used for shipping or storage, they are often discarded. Because of this, people all over the world are starting to use them to build their own useful items.

The best part about wood pallets is that they are typically *free*, or at least offered at an extremely affordable rate. They're just about everywhere, where there is civilization.

It's actually kind of sad to think that so much is produced and wasted. But finding ways to reuse these types of materials, instead of throwing them out, is a great way to make a change. Even recycling material required more processing, power consumption, and producing its own waste materials.

Upcycling could be considered the one true way to recycle without causing more waste in the process.

Safety First

It is important to note that pallets are used to carry all mananer of things, some of which are dangerous for human contact. You can never really know for sure where a pallet has been, and that leaves you open to possible harm. Of course, most pallets are not used around anything harmful, but it's still important to be aware. Specially treated pallets can also be an issue, and they might be harmful if burnt, cut, or even handled with bare skin.

When you go to pick up some pallets, look to see if they have had anything spilled on them. Since pallets are used again and again, before they are too worn to be thrown away, all types of things could happen to them. Aim to obtain clean looking pallets, without any stains that you can see.

Wooden pallets which are used to transport food can be contaminated with things like e.coli and listeria, according to the Consumers Leage (NCL).

Have you found some stain free pallets? That's great, but you still need to check what

markings, stamps, etchings, brandings, or painted areas there are on them. If there are none of the above things on a pallet, it should be clean and safe to use. Pallets that are not treated with chemicals, and are used for domestic trasport, do not legally have to be marked.

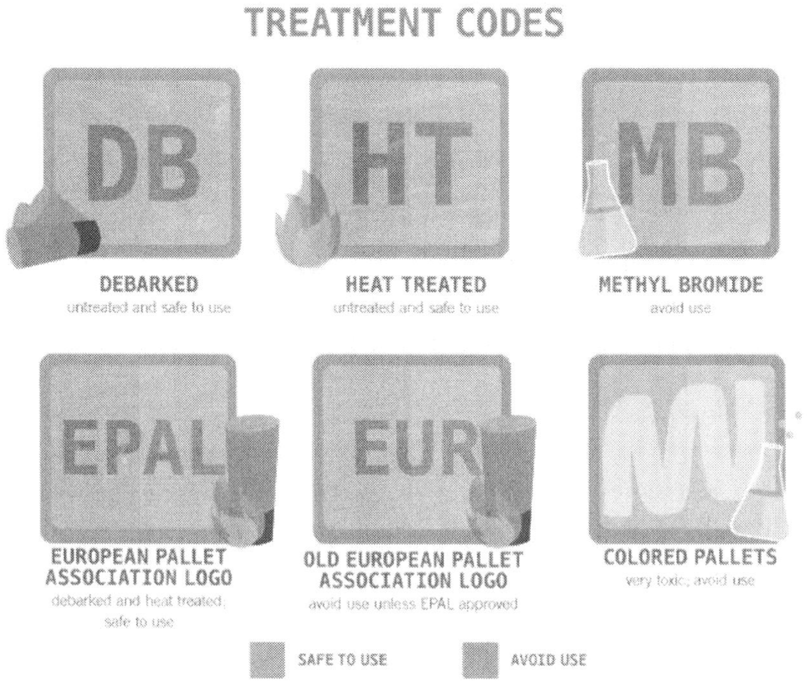

TREATMENT CODES

DEBARKED — untreated and safe to use

HEAT TREATED — untreated and safe to use

METHYL BROMIDE — avoid use

EUROPEAN PALLET ASSOCIATION LOGO — debarked and heat treated, safe to use

OLD EUROPEAN PALLET ASSOCIATION LOGO — avoid use unless EPAL approved

COLORED PALLETS — very toxic; avoid use

SAFE TO USE   AVOID USE

Types of Pallets

There are a number of different pallet designed. Some of them aren't even made of wood, although we won't be worrying about that type in this book. The most commonly seen pallet design is the two-way entry pallet. These consist of a series of planks on one side that make a flat surface. There are thicker pieces of wood in the center to provide some strength and to space the top and bottom apart. On the other side is another series of planks that make the bottom (or top, depending on which side is facing up). There are planks on two of the sides, meaning that a forklift could on pick this type of pallet up from two directions.

There are also four-way entry pallets, which don't have these sides.

The other pallets designs are not that different. They vary in size and how they're put together. But a pallet is generally a mostly flat wood structure, which acts as a floor for goods to be moved on.

It's recommended that you go for something like the two common types mentioned here, if you have a choice. Packing crates are also useful, as you will see in one of the projects in this book. In the end, pallets are a way to get free wood, and you can get pretty creative when using them, no matter what design you get your hands on.

Where to Get Pallets

The main thing preventing many people from building with wood pallets, is being unable to actually find any. Where can you find pallets that are most likely to be clean and free from hazardous substances? Here are some of the best places to look, the next time you deside you'd like to build something new with some free materials.

Animal Feed Store. This is one of the top places to look. They often have soft wood pallets, which are used to carry food; that means they're not likely to contain any toxis or poisonous substances.

Landscaping Businesses. The plants, sod, shrubs, and trees that are reguarly hauled around by landscapers need pallets for transportation. Just stay away from the types that are colored and used for oving fertilizers, or other harmful materials.

Newspaper Delivery Centers. These places, as well as the distribution centers, ship some pretty harmless goods on their pallets. If you ask one of the managers, or even a driver, they might be able to give you permission to take some of their old pallets.

Local Construction Sites. Residential sites will have pallets that have been used for carrying cement, bricks, joining compounds, and other things that are not toxic. Don't just go and help yourself though, or you will likely be breaking the law. Ask the builder if they have any pallets that they no longer need. Avoid the bigger, commercial sites, because they're more likely to have harmful pallets.

Preparing Your Pallets

Be careful when you're getting your pallets ready for building. It would be a shame to go through all the work to get some usable pallets, only to wreck them during preperation. Here are some tools and methods that you might find invaluable while trying to dismantle or otherwise use your pallet wood.

These techniques are listed in order of desperation. Try the first method, and only move down the list if that doesn't work.

You can use a hammer with a flat claw attached, a cat's paw, or a pry bar to simply take the pallet apart. Use a solid block of wood to brace each section as you do this, so that you don't break it.

A nail punch can be used to drive the nail out of the wood, instead of pulling on it.

Cutting the shank of a nail can work, allowing you to then pull the rest out more easily. If you can loosen the nail enough to do this, you might be able to use this technique.

Drilling works well if you don't have any other option. Just get a metal drill and use it to drill out those stubborn nails.

When you just can't get the pieces of wood apart, a simple, clean cut might be the best solution. This will leave the nails still imbedded in the wood, however.

Coffee Mug Rack

If you're an avid lover of coffee, tea, or even hot chocolate, this coffee mug rack project is sure to be a favorite. It shouldn't take long, depending on your level of skill, and the tools that you have. It might be a great idea to involve your kids with this one as well, provided you supervise and do the heavier steps for them.

You don't necessarily have to use these instructions to build a cup holder. If you'd prefer, you can change the distance of the hooks, and create a pot holder, or even somewhere you store a range of kitchen items. This might be a good idea for people who are short on space, and want a cheap, attractive solution to that problem.

Before you get started, you might want to go over your pallet with a power washer. After all, you will be hanging your drinking mugs on it, and probably keeping it where you prepare and store food.

What You'll Need
One pallet

Wood screws

Hooks for holding your mugs

Paint and stencil for writing a sign on your rack (if you want to)

Sandpaper

Tape measure

Right angle ruler

Pencil

Circular saw

Safety goggles

Cordless drill

Screwdriver

Making This Project

You're not going to need an entire pallet, unless you have one that's particularly tiny. Choose which section of the pallet looks best, including the mid joint to keep it stable.

Use the pencil to mark with the right angle ruler, where you'd like to cut. The size of the area you mark will decide how large your rack will be.

Cut your pallet with the circular saw (although a hand saw will do the job, at a slower speed). This will give you basically a miniature pallet, with a structure that holds together well.

Sand the wood down, especially where you cut it. Make sure it's all smooth and free of splinters and sharp areas.

You can paint something like "COFFEE" or "MUGS" at the top, as shown in the image. Use a stencil, or just free-draw it with a pain brush. It's okay to do this in a rustic way, because that's the whole image behind using pallets, after all.

Using a tape measure or ruler, take your pencil and mark out where you'd like to place your hooks. Making it even is a good idea to start with, but you might want to get creative with your placements. It doesn't really matter if it's not perfect, because of the hand crafted nature of this rack.

Predrill holes where the screws will go in, but make the drill bit a little smaller than the actual screws.

Using your screws, attach the hooks for the cups.

Your drinks mug rack is now complete!

Deck Chair

This next project could be quite useful for anyone who wants to invite friends over for a grill session, or just to sit around a nice fire, but doesn't have anywhere for people to sit. You don't want to take your indoor chairs outside, and risk getting them dirty or wet.

These "Adirondack" style chairs are perfect for building with pallet wood, and they are not as difficult as you might think. People tend to assume that any useful furniture has to be incredibly difficult, and expensive to make. That's certainly not the case.

Keep in mind that these chairs are going to be seeing a lot of weather. They are, after all, most likely going to be left outside all of the time. Use weather resistent screws, glew, paint, and anything else you think might be ruined by the rain, wind, snow, etc.

What You'll Need

Pallets (one per chair should be enough, depending on how big yours are)

Screws (for outdoor use)

Wood glue (water proof)

Jig saw

Compound miter saw

Power drill

Driver

Table saw

Belt sander

Palm sander

Safety goggles

If you're missing some of these items, such as the more expensive power tools, you can often make do with the hand powered equivalents. Just be prepared to put in some good, ol' fashioned elbow grease.

Making This Project

You'll need to cut some plank pieces from your pallet. Since all pallets might be a different size and shape, you'll need to use your own judgement here. Take a look at the above picture to see how to put the frame together.

When you're happy that the pieces are the right size for you, and whoever will be sitting on your chairs, glue and then screw this basic frame together. You can use clamps to hold it all together until the glue dries, but the screws should work fine here.

To make your seat back, take two pieces of wood to make the accross section, and then line up plank pieces to make a comfy flat part for your back. See how the top of the seat back is rounded? You can cut this to your own desire, to get this effect.

The seat part is made by laying plank pieces over the seat part of the frame, which you make earlier.

Now you can attach your seat back to the frame.

Sand everything down and paint or finish the wood as you desire.

Shipping Crate Storage Table

Okay, this next project is not technically a pallet build. However, since people all over the world have gotten into upcycling and the DIY spirit, other things, like packing crates, have been commonly used. And they're not that different from pallets. If you can find some packing crates, why not use them in their already made form to create something new? The best part about this table, is you can open the top and keep things inside, out of the way, but always close to hand.

The best part about using packing crates for a build, is that the basic shape is already there for you. All you have to do is get creative, and add the finishing touches.

What You'll Need
4 blocks for the legs, or wheels is you prefer to have a moving table

2 Hinges

A handle to use on your lid

A sheet of plywood to act as the lid (this should be a little wider than the top of your crate

Screwdriver or power drill

Screws

Sandpaper

Paint or finisher (your choice here, but something water resistent might help with any unwanted spills on your table)

Making This Project
You will want to sand down your whole crate, before you get started. Make sure there are no nasty splinters or edges that someone could hurt themselves on.

This is also a good time to finish your crate, or add weather proofing if you would like to do so.

Using your screws and drill, attach the wooden legs, or wheels, to the bottom of your crate. Place these near the corners of the crate, but leave a little space from the edge, in order to add strength.

Take your hinges and attach them to your piece of plywood, near the corners, along the length.

Attach your hinged piece of plywood to the crate, as shown in the final images.

Attach your handle to the plywood lid, on the opposite side of the hinges.

Minimal Pallet Bed

Have you noticed that actual bed frames are becomming more and more rare these days? It seems that people would rather buy the box types. These do look fine, but they don't exactly make moving easy, and storage is a nightmare as well. Some people would also rather have a regular bed frame, so that they can store things under the bed, like boxes or folding furniture. Why waste that space, after all?

Since you're going to be sleeping on this project, with possibly two people as well, it's important that it is sturdy. This can begin when you pick up your pallets. Make sure that you buy pallets with strong wood, and no obvious weak points. Even if you make a great bed, inferior quality material could make it creaky, unstable, or just unable to hold your weight.

What You'll Need
Three or four pallets, depending on size (the main surface of the bed should be made up of two pallets, if they're big enough)

A saw (power saws are easier, but hand saws work fine)

Wood screws

Power drill

Sand paper or power sander

Paint or varnish (if you like)

Making This Project

Did you find pallets that are the right size for your bed's surface, without being cut?

That is preferable, so nice work! Otherwise, you'll nedd to cut them down to the right size.

Measure how long you need the bed, and how wide, so that you and your partner will be comfortable. Leave the support beams of wood that hold the pallet planks together in tact, or you will have very unstable pallets to work with.

With the extra pallet or two you gathered, take some planks and use them to reinforce the main two planks. Do this by attaching them accross the planks of the pallets, underneath where they'll face up.

Now you can have some fun and sand down all of your wood (don't get too excited). A power sander is definitely recommended for this arduous task.

Fit the pallets together and mark where you'll need to drill holes for your screws. Do this with the soon-to-be tops of the pallets face down, to keep it even.

Drill holes where your screws will go in.

Take some blocks from your extra pallets, or make blocks out of pallet planks. These will be your legs, so drill holes where you'll attach them.

Now's the time to paint everything, or varnish, if you want to.

Glue and screw the parts together, so it look like the image below. You're done!

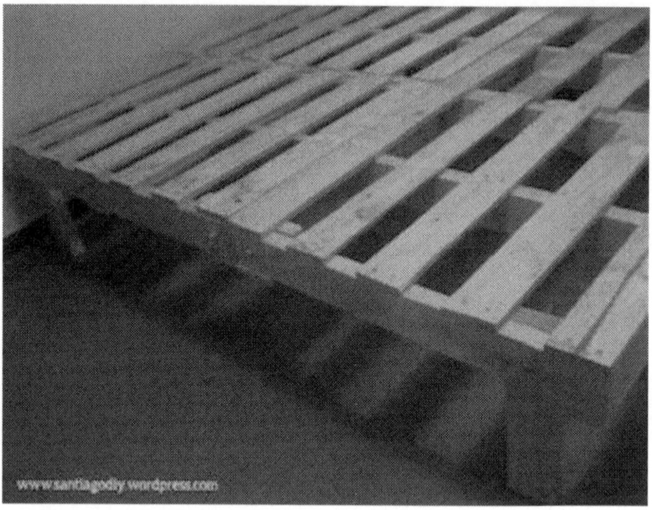
www.santiagodiy.wordpress.com

Food Serving Cart on Wheels

You might have enough furniture in your sitting area. But do you have somewhere to keep things that you are using? This could include stuff for drinks and snacks that you have already served, or are waiting to serve soon. Maybe you don't want to clutter up your coffee or dining table with bits and pieces that you don't actually need right now. This is where a handy little serving cart, on wheels of course, can make your life a whole lot easier.

Even if you don't use it very often, this cart is great for keeping decorative items. It is a very easy build as well, requiring a small amount of materials.

What You'll Need

A pallet, and it doesn't have to be very big

Hammer and nails

4 wheels for the bottom

Pain or varnish (your choice)

Sandpaper

Making This Project

Take a look at the below image, of the basic structure turned upside down, if you're not sure about how to put this together.

You'll need to basically take your pallet apart and use the pieces to craft this rolling cart "from scratch". This makes it a good project to build with non-pallet wood, if you have any, or if you can't find any pallets.

Put your top frame together, using two lengths of wood and joining then with two shorter pieces. Check the image to get a better idea.

Using short lengths of pallet planks, create a top surface over this top frame.

Repeat the previous two steps to make the bottom storage surface.

Use four lengths of wood to create the legs, and attach everything together.

Add your wheels on the bottom of the legs.

Sand everything down, finish it, and paint it (if you like).

Pallet Plank Shelf

This is a really simple, but extremely practical, type of shelf. The best part is that you can whip one one in next to no time. You don't even need an entire pallet to make this one. In fact, you can use any old plank of wood that you find. Pallet wood is, of course, one of the cheapest options for the DIYer on a budger.

These shelves are great to put up where you don't have a lot of space for an actual shelving unit.

What You'll Need
Two pallet planks that are at least as long as you want the shelf to be

A power saw (hand saw will do nicely for this project)

Sand paper

Paint or varnish (your choice once again here)

Wood screws

Hooks for clothes hanging section

Tape measure

Picture hangers

Making This Project
Measure the wall where you wish to put your shelf (or hold the planks against the wall and mark where you'll need to cut)

Cut both of your planks to the right length

Using your drill and the wood screws, attach the two planks together in a 90 degree fashion, lengthwise (look at the finished image if you're unsure of this step). Drill holes for your screws first, to prevent splitting of the wood.

Mark where you want to put your hooks. If you don't have real hooks, you can use anything of similar shape, like cupboard knobs (see the image). You can place these evenly, or however you like.

Now that your holes are marked, it's time to drill some holes, and then attach your hooks.

The screws or bolts that you've used to attach the hooks might stick out of the back of the shelf. You can't put it up on the wall like that, so you'll need to (carefully) saw the excess metal off at the back. Smooth this down with sandpaper so it won't scratch your walls up.

Now you can attach the picture hangers on the back of the shelf, spaced far enough to provide a lot of balance. If you don't have these, you can get away with using some strong wire. Make sure it's not going to break and let the shelf drop.

Now you can hang your shelf, as you would a big painting.

Rustic Drinks Cooler

If you'd like to learn to make your own outdoor-style cooler that's rustic, and made from pallets, this is the perfect project for you. You'll only need one variety of saw for this build, making it great for people who have a limited amount of tools. Once you wrap your head around the tutorial, and you have all of the required gear together, this project should just take a day to put together.

What You'll Need

At least 5 pallets

A power washer (if you can't scrub the wood by hand)

Dremel saw

Your cooler of choice, of the right size, of course

Impact drill

Wood working pencil (or a normal pencil)

Measuring tape

Screwdriver (flat head)

Hammer

Pliers

Prying bar

Wood screws (exterior type)

Strong bond wood glue

Bolts

Hinges

T-nuts

Bore drill bit

Bibb for hose

Handle

PVC coupling (some coolers won't require this)

A handle

Making This Project

Once you have your pallets, you will want to scrub them down, or preferably use a power washer to get them nice and clean. The wood will come up very nicely if you do use a power washer.

Remove the planks of wood from your pallets. Make sure that you have enonugh to cover the sides of the cooler, with the planks running horizontally.

Take off the wheels, handles, latches, and hinges from the cooler, and any other hardware parts that will get in the way when you put it into the wooden structure you'll be making next.

Your cooler is going to need four legs. Take 8 slats of wood (depending on how big yours are) and cut 32 inch length pieces.

Join 2 of your slacks together at 90 degrees length-wise, with screws and glue. Be sure to pre-drill before inserting screws, to avoid splitting the wood. Do this again, making two lips for the top lengths of your cooler.

Join the lips with two lengths of wood.

Measure the cooler's height and work out how many wood planks you'll need to make the sides.

To make a leg, join two lengths of wood at 90 degrees, as you did with the top lip. Make sure they're long enough to go from the top of the cooler to the ground, past the base of the cooler.

You can now join your top lip, sides pieces, and legs together, as in the image.

To make the lid, create two lips again, join them with short plank pieces, and use plank lengths to cover the top.

Attach the lid with your hinges and you are good to go!

Garden Planter

Are you yearning for something more in your garden than grass and maybe a few edge plants? How about being able to grow something that you can actually put to good use—like some fresh food?

This planter is a great idea for people who want to get into the hobby of gardening, especially people with children. Since you won't need much pallet wood, or any fancy tools and expertise, this is an especially fun project to do over the summer with kids.

By filling your planter with soil, and standing it over in an out-of-the-way place in the garden, you can reap the rewards of fresh produce. Okay, so you're not going to become self-sufficient with just one, or even a few, of these planters. The real reward comes from growing something yourself, and knowing where it came from. They also look great, and are very stylish right now.

What You'll Need
One pallet per planter (with six or nine pallet planks across the top)

Hammer

Nails

Hand saw (although a power saw will make things a lot easier)

Soil, furtilizer, bedding material, etc. (this is up to you)

Seeds, saplings, etc. (this one's also up to you)

Making This Project
Take a look at the below image to get an idea of where to cut, before you begin.

Cut your pallet into three equal pieces, going across the joining pieces of wood. Check out the below picture if you're not sure how to do this.

You should have two end pieces, and one from the middle. Split this middle piece if half, taking the top and bottom apart.

Cut the end pieces so that they appear as in the image as well.

Attach your sides using your hammer and nails, and use those extra pieces you cut off the create a bottom. Remember, this doesn't have to be water tight or anything. In fact, drainage for the soil is essential.

You should have some blocks of wood left over. Use these to create little feet for the whole structure.

You should now have a nice planter. Fill it up with some garden bedding material at the bottom, for filler and drainage. You can put your soil up near the top, along with whatever you want to plant.

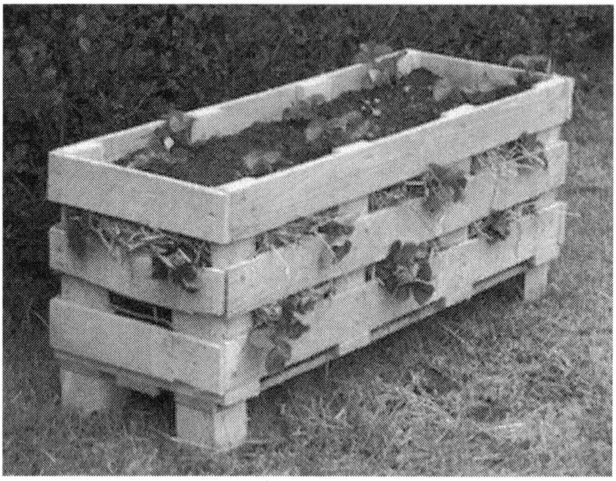

Two Seater Chair

Depending on how handy you are, and what tools you have at your disposal, it should be realistically feasible to build this chair in just a few hours.

Are you after something new and unique, with a heavy rustic charm? This little chair is not something you will find in the stores, so why not build it yourself?

If you are in the mood for creating some more crafts, this chair goes great with some burlap sack cushions, as seen in the final image at the end of this plan.

This build is going to require a few extra bits of wood, which might be difficult to find from a pallet. Of course, that depends on the pallets you have, and how you can use them to your advantage.

What You'll Need
Two pallets of roughly the same size

Four pieces of wood to use as the legs (you will need durable legs for this build, sorry)

Two boards to use as the arms

Power drill

Wood screws

Sand paper

Saw (power saw is best, but hand will do as well)

Making The Project
Sand down your pallets to remove rough edges. One of your pallets is going to be your seat, and the other one is going to be the backrest of the chair.

Attach your legs to the seat pallet, on the shorter sides, as in the image of the finished chair. You'll want to attach it about 1/3 of the way up the legs. This will give you somewhere to attach the arm rests, as well as long lift off the ground.

Attach your arm rest boards to the tops of the legs.

Attach your backrest pallet to the seat pallet.

Pain and finish if you like, or leave it all looking nice and rustic!

You're done with your simple pallet chair. Add cushions as you like, for comfort.

Conclusion

It can certainly be a lot of fun making things out of wood pallets. You don't have to stop with the plans and designs contained in this book. There are plenty of ideas floating around online as well. Once you get into the spirit of upcycling, you will be amazed a the number of things you can create, and using items that might have otherwise been thrown away.

So, why spend hundred of dollars on new furtniture, which is probably just flat packed, wobbly, and not very nice looking? The alternative might be to spend loads more on items to fill your home. Or ... you can just learn how to do a little DIY and create things yourself.

Please remember that the instructions laid out in this book are meant to be used by adults, or under the careful supervision of adults. When you are using pallet wood, it's always important to assume that it might be treated with harmful materials, like chemicals and poisons.

25 Woodworking Projects

Introduction

Most of the people like to choose DIY woodworking projects to décor your home. The reason is that they are easy to make on the one side while on the other side they are fun as well. DIY stands for "Do It Yourself" so it means that there are such projects that you can try by yourself without taking help of anyone. This is very true and all the projects that you will learn ahead are so easy and exiting that you will love to start them right after learning them.

Woodworking projects or ideas are equally popular among each age group. The reason is that wood is such a material that increases the beauty of your home while on the other side its easy to work with it. Other materials like metals and plastic are difficult to handle and work with but wood on the other side is relatively easy to handle and work with in an amazing way. That's the reason due to which beginners also find woodworking projects a fun when they start.

Due to realistic and decent look that wood gives to homes, people choose it decorate every corner of their homes. If you don't have a lot of space and still you want to decorate your home with woodworking projects that you can do two things in this regard. First you need to declutter the things that you are not using since three years. The second thing that you can do is that go vertical with wood so that even in the small space you may décor your home in a perfect way.

Usually some people have less space in the kitchen, study area or even in patio. So they always look for such ideas that help them to decorate every single area. Some people usually don't have enough space for studying. Here in the few chapter you will learn everything that how to get maximum out of your small space.

Chapter 1 – 15 Incredible Woodworking Projects To Decorate Your Indoors

In this chapter you will learn some incredible woodworking ideas to decorate your indoor. The below mentioned DIY woodworking projects will enable you to utilize your skills and make marvelous things for your indoors. If you have some idea other than these projects then still you can utilize that idea. But these projects are the basic ones that will help you to make complicated things with great ease. Let's learn these projects to decorate indoors!

Woodworking Project 01: Make white indoor sofa set:

You can make amazing white indoor sofa set for your indoor. White sofa sets are the choice of most of the people because they look simple and adorable. If you have sufficient space in your home or want to replace the existing sofa then this woodworking project to make a sofa can prove very vital for you.

To make this simple at stylish white sofa set you need few things. For instance you need to get some wooden pallets, cozy cushion, tyres, screws etc. You will also need all those materials that are otherwise required in woodworking projects to make work easier. They may include different types of saws, drill machines, nails, sandpaper, paint etc. So far this pallet white sofa set is concerned you can easily make it by putting little bit efforts.

The white pallet sofa as shown in the picture has eight seating. But you can make sofa with more or less seating as well. To make white sofa you need to gather and secure the pallets in a way as shown in picture. This design is fairly simple and the beginners can also make this one with bit ease. Next to it get the pallets to make white table for this sofa set. Join the pallets and attach the wheels as well.

When you are done with joining the pallets both for table and sofa then paint them in white and set it to dry. (You can choose any other paint color but here we are focusing on white due to this project requirement). After paint get some cozy cushions and put on the sofa. Here note that this is a white sofa therefore you need to get white covers for the cushions to give it an elegant look. When its ready place it in your living room and enjoy comfortable seating.

Woodworking Project 02: Make vintage pallet sectional sofa:

You can make this vintage pallet sectional sofa by yourself. If you have less space in your home and want to get a cool and vintage look then you can for this idea. This vintage sofa is a part of woodworking project that is easy and inexpensive as well.

To make this vintage pallet sofa you need to get some pallets. Secure the pallets to make the base of sectional sofa. We also called it L shape sofa. After making the base you need to get the mattress for your sectional sofa. The size of the mattress and sofa should be same. Here the cover of the mattress is black. After that get some cushions according to your needs and place them on the sectional sofa. Here we used some large and small cushions in different colors. You can also do it.

To make this sectional sofa we recommend you that sew the cushion covers by yourself. If you have some pieces of cloth at your home then bring them in use. In this way multicolour cushions will look more adorable for indoors. We avoided paint in this project to give more vintage look to this sofa set.

Woodworking Project 03: Join pallets and hang different things:

You can make this woodworking project to hang most of your things that are placed haphazardly in your room. Often your children are too lazy to keep the things in place. So you can make one of such pallet projects to keep the things in one place. This is simple DIY project that will look so enchanting in your room. This is also a pallet project that goes vertical in your small or even big room. You can hang your scarfs, mufflers, shoulder bags and hats over there. So keep your room tidy and go for this project. This will also decorate your walls if you go with it.

To make this you need to get 9 wooden pallets. Secure the pallets in a way as shown in the picture such as place (secure with wall of your room) three pallets horizontally at the back then join the six pallets vertically with three pallets. You can notice that the two pallets at both sides are somewhat wide while the others in the middle are not. The reason is the wide pallets can be used to hang some other large items.

After secure the pallets with nails, next you need to paint the pallets. To make them colourful and cool you can paint each pallet in different colors as shown in the picture. When the paint is properly dried then hang your different things with it to save space in your room.

Woodworking Project 04: Make pallet sofa with some storage:

You can also make a pallet sofa with some storage capacity. Often you have plenty of things in your home that you can't place anywhere. So in such cases you want to go for such woodworking projects that save space on one hand while on the other side they look highly beautiful for indoors. One of such idea is to make a multipurpose sofa. You can make storage sofa for your kid's room as shown in the picture. Your children will love to sit and study on such sofa.

To make this incredible storage sofa you need few pallets, a sofa mattress and three cushions. First join the pallets in a way as shown in the picture. Paint the pallets or not, it's entirely up to you. Next to it you need to place sofa mattress over the pallets. Use the one that covers its back side as well. Then place three cushions over it to get a comfortable sitting. Now place your extra things in the storage places that you have made. This storage sofa provides you different storage sections. So you can place your different things in different sections. Hence most of space in your room is left for other important things.

Woodworking Project 05: Project for kitchen:

While decorating other parts of your home how you can forget or ignore your kitchen. Your kitchen is an important part of your home. Hence there is also a need to decorate your home in an amazing way. There are a lot of complicated projects for your kitchen that are expensive and difficult to make. In addition some other woodworking projects are also there that can make your kitchen look so stylish and adorable. You can see one of such DIY inexpensive project in the image.

Most of the times you want to save space in your kitchen, so you often look for options that are simple and stylish. To make this woodworking project you need wooden boards. Get three wooden boards and make proper holes in them as shown in the picture then get pieces of cloth and bind it with the wood. The holes that you made in the board will help you in hanging go vertical and hand the boards with the hooks. Then place the spoons, forks and other such things in them. Hence this woodworking project for kitchen will not only help you to keep the things in an arranged way but also it will give fascinating look to your kitchen as well.

Woodworking Project 06: Make vase and other decoration pieces:

You can make a lot of amazing and unique things with woods. Wood has countless uses and the limit is skies. Besides furniture you can also make a lot of wood things to decorate your home and surroundings. There are a lot of decoration pieces that are solely made of wood. Either use pallets or logs or get some unique design by crafting the wood, you are going to get amazing decoration pieces. Place them on the table or secure them with the wall, all of them will give a fabulous look to your home.

To make this vase you need some small wood logs. Cut them in proper size. The diameter should be 2 inches while the length can also be 1.5-2.5 inches. Keep the length same. Now get some vase or use some old bucket and join the logs with it by using wood gum that will secure the small logs with it. Now place some flowers of your desire in it. This wooden vase can be placed on the side table. Moreover it's also a good idea to use it for outdoor tables.

Now check the following wall mounted design. This design is also good to go with. You can start this simplest woodworking project to decorate your home walls. Cut and arrange the wood as shown in the picture. Before mounting with the wall use a glass in the middle as shown. This woodworking project will decorate the walls of your home in really an amazing way. So why don't you try it?

Woodworking Project 07: Make indoor pallet swing chair:

After the long hectic day you want to release your stress and tension. One of the easiest thing that you can do in this regard is that make an indoor pallet swing chair for your home by yourself. This is really a great woodworking project for those who love swing. But before starting this project make sure that the roof of your home is strong enough to support this swing chair and your weight as well. If the roof is not that much strong then don't choose it for indoors rather choose it for outdoors.

To make this indoor swing chair you need to gather and secure some pallets. Paint them in white and place a cozy white mattress over it. But before placing the mattress you need to do some other things. Such as use some rope or metal chair to fasten this swing chair with the roof (or with tree in case of outdoors).

Woodworking Project 08: Make Pallet pot rack for your kitchen:

This is another simple project to decorate your kitchen and save a lot of space. One thing that is missing in this project is that the pallets are not painted. But to make this pot rack more stylish and astonishing you can paint these pallets in the same or different colors.

To make this pallet pot rack you need to gather some pallets so that and secure them in an appropriate way. Moreover don't forget to attach hooks with it so that you may fasten it with the walls using a strong chain. Again I will recommend to paint the pallets but if you want a rustic look then this project is still good to go with.

Woodworking Project 09: Make rusting pencil holders:

You can also decorate your study table by making rusting pencil holders. If you want to make something for your children by yourself then don't forget to try this project. These rusting pencil holders look fantastic when placed on the study table. Moreover it becomes convenient for your children to place and take out pencils out of these pencil holders. In addition your child will be finding to the required color by just rotating the holder. So help your child in finding the right pencil or pencil color of his choice by making this pencil holder.

This pencil holder is so easy to make as you just need a log. Get an appropriate sized log that may fit in perfectly on the study table. Moreover it should not be so heavy. The reason is that sometimes there comes a need to take it anywhere in the home, because more often children don't like studying at one place. So to make this pencil holders get a log and make some holes using drill machines. The holes should be deep enough to hold the pencils.

Woodworking Project 10: Make indoor daybed:

You can make this pallet daybed for your children. This indoor daybed can decorate your space in a very good way. This daybed is good and can be used for so many purposes. Your children can sleep and study on this bed. It can serve a lot of other functions as well.

To make this daybed you need to get a lot of equal sized pallets. These pallets are should be clean and without any damage, because otherwise they will not last longer. For daybeds you need only to make a base. Make proper base and paint in white. Then place white mattress over it. Use some pillows and cushions to give it a complete look.

Woodworking Project 11: Make indoor coffee table:

You can also make pallet coffee table for your home. Coffee tables can also add the beauty to your home. The coffee table as shown in the picture is rusted. It means that the pallets are not painted. This coffee table has storage place as well where you can place some other things such as books, magazines etc.

To make this coffee bed you need to gather and secure the pallets. Secure them in such a way as shown in the picture. Make some storage places underneath and use wheels to make this coffee table moveable. This is completely rustic and such type of wood doesn't need to be painted. The height of this coffee table is not too high. This can be placed indoors to fill your extra space. Place vase on the table and make it more stylish.

Woodworking Project 12: Make pallet sectional sofa and matching table for indoor:

You can make this pallet sectional sofa and matching table along with it. This sectional sofa is an amazing woodworking project to meet your indoor needs. This sectional sofa is so wide and cozy where your guests will love to sit. This seating arrangement is good for six people. After joining the pallets use mattresses and cushions to make them cozy.

When your sectional sofa is ready then next move to the table. The table should also have same height and width. After making the table with pallets join wheels. After that get a proper glass and place it on the top of the table. You can place lamp, magazines etc. on this. This pallet sofa set is really good to decorate your indoors.

Woodworking Project 13: Make book shelves:

There are a lot of woodworking ideas to make book shelves. You can make wooden book shelves for your home in amazing way. If you have a lot of space at your disposal then you can decide a corner where you make wooden book shelves. But if you don't have enough space then you have to decide for book shelves out of your room. There are a lot of ideas for this as well. The one idea as shown in the image is such that you would love to try. These book shelves are made under the stairs where you can sit and study for long hours. Usually such place goes in waste as you don't use this. But making wooden shelves in such a place is really a great idea. In this way you will place your books on the one side while on the other side you will be able to decorate your home in appropriate way.

To make such wooden shelves you need to get wood. For instance you can also use wooden pallets to make these shelves. Arrange woods in a way as shown in the picture and then paint them. You can also see that there is also study table in front where you can place your PC or laptop. Left to this area there are some drawers where you can place your important things. Thus this book shelves idea to decorate your home is really great and easy as well.

Woodworking Project 14: Make pallet teen girl bed:

If you want to make pallet teen girl bed then you can go for the one that is shown in the picture. The color combination is also too good that teen girls love. This teen bed is without legs. But you can construct in a way that it is above the floor/ground. This is such an amazing bed that your teen girl will love to sleep on it.

To make this bed you need some pallets of equal size. You can notice this bed is made in two pallet steps. First make the ground case using some large pallets and paint it. After that, make a small case of pallets with same technique and materials. But the upper case of the bed should be relatively small. For this purpose use pallets of small sized. After that, paint well in white. Then get the mattress in pin and place the cushions in white. This color combination and style is really adorable and your teen girl is likely to admire your efforts.

Woodworking Project 15: Make pallet wall panel:

Pallet wall panel look really amazing in homes. You can also make beautiful pallet wall panel by yourself but remember this project required a lot of patience and time as well. If you got pallets of right size then it's easy to mount them on the wall. But if some pallets are too large then you have to cut them each time before mounting them on the walls.

To make this wall panel you need to get a lot of pallets according to width and height of your wall. In this image pallets are mounted on the entire wall but you can mount them to cover half of the wall. Mounts these pallets on the wall in such a way that whole wall is covered. After mounting them you can use oil paints to make them more beautiful.

In short, these are some woodworking projects that will help you to decorate your space in an amazing way. You can try one or all of the projects to make your home more beautiful. These are some projects that can meet your indoor needs very perfectly.

Chapter 2 – 10 Woodworking Projects To Decorate Your Outdoor Space

Your backyard garden or patio is an integral part of your home so you can't avoid it. There is a need to decorate your outdoor space as well. This task can easily be accomplished if you follow the following mentioned projects. These projects are highly marvelous and you can try them with bit ease. Let's learn these woodworking projects!

Woodworking Project 01: Make outdoor pallet table:

If you just want to make an outdoor pallet table then it's also a good idea. If you have metal chairs and want to make pallet table then you can start this project. This woodworking pallet table project is very easy. All you need to get some pallets to start this project.

To make this pallet table you need to gather pallets of equal size. This outdoor pallet table has some storage place as well. So while joining the pallets make sure that you are joining them in the same way as shown in the picture. Next to it get four wheels and attach them at the bottom. In this way you will be able to move your table easily here and there in your backyard garden.

Woodworking Project 02: Outdoor pallet sitting plan:

This pallet outdoor sitting plan is going to meet your outdoor needs. Working on this woodworking project is time consuming but once you are done with it, you will get really fabulous results. This is a cozy sitting plan in white and blue combination. So for summers there is no great outdoor sitting plan than this.

To take start for this woodworking project get some pallets, nails and paint. Secure the pallets in appropriate way as revealed in the image. This set has sofa, table and a daybed. So this is a complete woodworking projects that caters your outdoor needs. After securing the pallets for daybed, table and sofa, you need to paint them. To paint the table you need white paint color for base and for top case use blue paint. After that, cover its top with glass. On the other hand use only white paint for the daybed and sofa. When paint is dried place some cozy cushions on the top and back of the sofa and enjoy comfortable sitting in your backyard.

Woodworking Project 03: Make outdoor pallet fence:

You can also make fantastic an outclass pallet fence for your backyard garden or patio. This fence is really easy then any other woodworking project and it has so many advantages as well. First of all it separates the area of your garden so it works like partition. Secondly it keeps pets and other animals out of the garden so your plants and other things remain safe. Thirdly it adds the beauty to your patio. So going with such an amazing project is highly appreciated.

To create this pallet fence you need pallets and secure them in a way as shown in the image. But you can also change them according to the needs and size of your garden.

Woodworking Project 04: Make beautiful wall garden:

If you lack with sufficient space in your backyard garden then you can make this beautiful wall garden with wood. This will not only look beautiful but also you can place different pots in it as well. Place some vegetable plants and ornamental plants to make this garden more beautiful.

To make this wall garden you need some pallets. Get some pallets in extra-large size for the back and small pallets for the pots where you will place different plants. First join the long pallets and then arrange the pots in appropriate way as shown above. Hence you will get a real wall garden within few days.

Woodworking Project 05: Make comfy daybed for outdoor:

You can easily try this comfy outdoor daybed. This daybed will meet your needs and you will love to sit there during your leisure time. The comfy daybed as shown in the picture is moveable. So when the outdoor whether is harsh you can move it easily to some safe place.

To get this you need some pallets, four wheels, mattress, and cushions. Don't paint this comfy sofa and give it rusting look. If you are using if for summers then keep the covers in light colors while for the winters you can get the dark colors for cushions.

Woodworking Project 6: Sectional sofa and moveable table for outdoor:

If you want to decorate your outdoor space then you can go for this outdoor sectional sofa and moveable table. The paint colors and cushions are good for summer. While moveable table for outdoor is also a good choice. You can take it anywhere in your patio.

To make this sectional arrangement combine pallets in a right way. Then place multicolour cushions and on it. Besides you can also make storage places in this sectional sofa. Enjoy comfortable sitting with your family and friends on this pallet outdoor sectional sofa.

Woodworking Project 7: Make bar with stools for outdoor:

You can decorate your outdoor space area with this bar table and stools. This is also a somewhat easy project that can meet your outdoor needs. You can have fun with your friends in the evening while sitting on such an arrangement. This outdoor bar arrangement is similar to the arrangement as you see in different clubs and casinos.

Firs make the bar with pallets and paint it. Use blue paint color and keep the top simple. On the top you can use oil paints to protect it. Next to make stools while keeping the size of the bar in mind. Without proper measurement you will either make too big or too small tools. So get an appropriate size for both things.

Woodworking Project 8: Make pallet bench and gabion table:

This is another amazing outdoor project for your garden. With some pallets you can make this beautiful arrangement for your backyard garden or patio. When its complete you can place a vase and different other things on such table. This is highly a creative way that you can opt for your outdoor especially your children will love to find such an arrangement. This woodworking project is not that much cozy but it can decorate your patio in really an amazing way. So find a proper place in your backyard for it or else you can make such arrangement for the centre of your garden.

Woodworking Project 9: Make place for pots:

This is another rusting arrangement for your outdoor. You can try this as well to meet your backyard decorative needs. Decide about any wall of your garden and make pallet wall panel. Then mount some pot cases with the wall. Make the pot cases with the pallets in the same size as shown below.

Woodworking Project 10: Make L shaped outdoor sitting plan:

This is really amazing outdoor L-Shaped sitting plan for your patio. Like other projects get some pallets and secure them in a way that they get L shape. Then paint the sofa and use mattress and cushions to make it cozy and comfortable. You can see the table is also made with the same wood.

In short these outdoor woodworking plans will decorate your outdoor space with less efforts and money. So learn to make such projects to decorate your patio or garden area.

Conclusion

You learned a lot about DIY woodworking projects that will help you to decorate your space. You learned a lot of easy and cozy woodworking projects that will add a unique spice to your woodworking experience. After learning these projects you are able now to decorate your indoor and outdoor. As in the first chapter of this DIY book you learned several woodworking projects that will help you to decorate your kitchen, living room and drawing room. You also learned that how you can take maximum out of the small space. So in regard you learned some woodworking projects that go vertical and save a lot of your space. Such vertical projects are decorative as well. While in the succeeding chapter you found some marvelous outdoor projects that will decorate your patio space. You learned how to make mounted pallet walls, pot cases, comfy sofas, outdoor daybeds, wall gardens and a lot of other woodworking projects. So now you are highly equipped with the versatile and adorable woodworking projects that will help you to make decoration pieces and furniture as well.

Wood Pallet Projects to Sell

Introduction

There is something utterly satisfying about making your own furniture. It takes you on a great learning experience and at the same time gives your house some of your own character. While trying to make the place your own, a great way to add a sense of belonging and a touch of personal style to your house is to take up some easy DIY projects.

One of the most beginner friendly DIY project is making wood pallet furniture. Not only is that beginner friendly but also light on the pocket. The great thing about wood pallet projects is that you can easily customize the project to suit your own level of advancement and experience with wood work. From simple clock and other decorative home accessories to big projects like coffee tables, chairs and even outdoor furniture, this book takes you through an exciting journey, guiding you every step of the way. In this book we have explored topics relating to home accessories, furniture and all that made from wood pallets. Not only are they an economically feasible option to decorate your home but they also prove to be very durable.

Furniture making can be without a doubt tricky business but in this book we have made it severely easy for you to follow pictorial as well as verbal guidelines that have been written in simple language to appeal to a large readership and to help anyone who wants to give this a try. Moreover, bear in mind that the projects discussed include tools and hardware and are not kid friendly. Precautions should be undertaken in order to endure safety of everyone involved.

Whether you are a new home owner or simply someone who is looking into renovation and redecorating your house to add home-feel to it, you have come to right place. So if you want to start turning your house into a home, let's begin building your own furniture, art and decor!

Chapter 1 – Pallet Home Accessories

A home without accessories is like a body without soul. It has no personality, no homey vibe and absolutely no character and charisma. To turn four walls into a living space that you can belong to and call your own you need to personalize it. To achieve that sense of affiliation and belonging there is no better way to add a touch of your style to your house so it mirrors your taste and personality. The best way to do that is add accessories that reflect your own style. And taking up a DIY to create your own home decor from scratch adds a cherry on top of the cake. In this chapter we will be taking you through three very easy to do projects using nothing but wood pallets from the comfort of your own home.

Project 1 – Wood Pallet Wall clocks

Wall clocks are a basic necessity of a household. Not only are the esthetically pleasing to the eye but also are a great way of adding some character and ambiance to your personal living space. They are useful and beautiful to look at which is what makes them a priority when thinking about wall decor.

As it happens, we walk into a rustic coffee shop which has vintage vibe to it and we think to ourselves, "Wow! I'd love to have some of that in my living room!"

Well, problem solved! A smart way to add those vintage decorative vibes is to add rustic decor. A big wood pallet wall clock on your master wall of the room gives it a tasteful style statement. Let's go through the steps you will need to follow to make a pallet clock.

Materials

- Wood pallet – Available at any thrift shops or yard sales
- Hammer

- Nails
- Glue
- Digits – to paste on the clock
- Paint

Procedure

1. The first step is to prepare the wood pallets. Depending on the condition of the pallet you purchased, you will need to dress it up a little bit. Using a hammer, take away rusty iron nails to separate the planks of the pallet.

2. Once the planks are out, arrange them in side by side as shown in the figure below to decide the shape you want your clock to be. It could be circular, rectangular, square depending on your choice. The graphical demonstration below shows the clock being made into a circular shape. This can easily be achieved by eyeballing the center and light hammering a nail at the center of your planks. A pencil is used to achieve a circular shape on the planks. This pencil sketch will serve as a guide for when the planks will be cut into your desired shape which s circular in this case.

3. Next, use a scroll saw or a jigsaw, depending on availability, to cut out the planks in the shape of a circle following the pencil sketch marks on the planks as your guideline. Once the planks are cut, use a combination of wood glue and nails to secure the planks together into circular shape for a sturdier framework. You will have something looking like the image below.

4. For extra strength, use some extra planks of wood to glue behind the clock so as to provide extra support to the frame and ensure that it is durable.

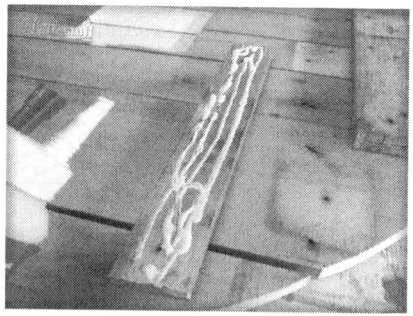

Now the next step is optional but is recommended to achieve that really neat and rustic look for your pallet clock. Using some diluted whitewash and sponge brush, go down the front of your clock to have a subdued vintage effect.

5. Now if you wanted a very basic, caveman's wooden pallet clock you are as good as done dressing the pallets. Just stick up some hands and numbers and you are good to go. But if you are someone who is willing to go that little extra mile to have a sterling masterpiece of a wooden pallet clock, I highly recommend this step. This is also an optional step but it never fails to give the pallet some personal touch of taste. Using any type of stencil, trace a shape right in the middle of the clock where the hands would be centered and paint that a different shade than the pallets to give your clock a pop of color. This is a great way to make the clock feel like the part of your room by matching the shade to your theme of interior.

6. Next, print out and cut large numbers to paste onto your clock as shown below. You can use a number of material to achieve this. It all just depends on your taste. Use stiff materials like cardboard, chart paper or Styrofoam to ensure durability.

7. Order 12 inch hands with high torque movement. These are available on many online shopping websites. Ensure they have high torque in accordance to your clock size.

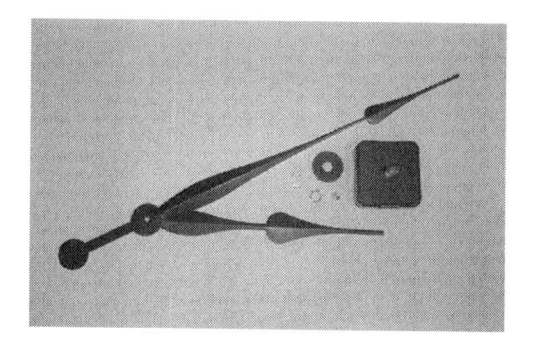

8. And voila! You just made yourself a pallet clock. Hang it in your living room and marvel at your handiwork! You can easily modify this project to suit the overall theme of whichever room are hanging the clock in. Some options for modification include painting the wooden planks, drawing creative art on them etcetera. The clock can also be modified to be made into other shapes like square, rectangular or even triangular. Really, it is all about getting creative.

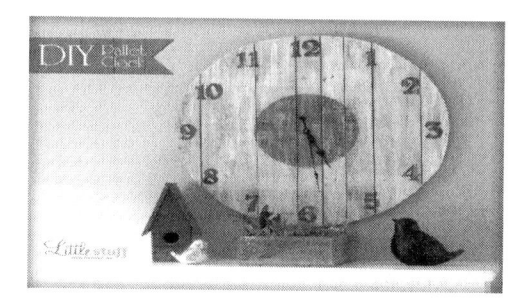

Project 2 – Pallet bookshelf

Bookshelves are a great addition to any wall. They artistically cover empty and boring walls whilst simultaneously giving you some well-articulated space for arranging decorative items, from photo frames to candles and books. This beautiful doubles as a creative spice rack for your kitchen or a bookshelf in the kids' room or even your own. It can also be utilized to energize a plain wall in the living room or any common area.

Materials

- Wooden Pallets of different sizes
- Wood glue
- Nails
- Paint (optional)

Procedure

1. Cut the planks in different sizes according to your desired lengths.

2. To make a three tier rectangular shelf as shown in the image above, three planks of varying sizes are required. One for the base, one for back and one for front. Cut them according to your preferred measurements.
3. Next, glue the planks together. Hammer a few iron nails in place for good support.
4. If you wish to make separations between each self, place a wooden partition a few inched long to divide into boxes.
5. If you wish to paint your shelf a bright color, paint over the planks and let dry overnight.
6. To hang the shelves onto the wall, drill two holes at the opposite ends of each shelving unit. Now drill holes in the wall where you want to place the shelves. Use measuring tape for accuracy. Put wall nails in the holes and hang your shelves.

Project 3 – Pallet Flag

This is an extremely easy and beginner friendly DIY project using wooden pallets. It can easily be completed in one day. And is also a fun way for the whole family to enjoy a day off together as a team. Let's begin!

Materials

- Wooden pallet
- Paint colors of depending on the country flag
- Nails/ wood glue

Procedure

1. *Paint* - As evident from the image above, this is a fairly simple project. All you need to do is print out an image of the desired flag. Next, keep the image in front of you for reference to avoid mistakes and hassle. Keeping the planks in front of you, start painting the planks according to the design of the flag.

2. Once you are done with painting the colors on to the planks, take two wooden planks long enough to cover the entire vertical length of all the colored planks. Glue and nail the two larger planks along the length of the painted planks that make up the flag. And you're done.

A rather playful and interesting spin on this project is to use this flag to make a coffee table with a twist. We will discuss that in further chapters.

Chapter 2 – Wood Pallet Furniture

Wood pallet is a very feasible and durable item to build home furniture on your own. Furniture is what gives character to a home. And materials like wood give a posh appearance. However, walking into a furniture store, you feel like you can never bring yourself to burden your pocket that much. We have a solution for you. Furniture made from wood pallets is durable, beautiful and gives a luxe persona to your living spaces. Here, we guide you step by step on how to build your very own furniture using nothing but wood pallets and very basic hardware. And the best part is that you do not even need high tech expertise to undertake one of these projects. We have got you covered. Just grab those wooden pallets and your tool box and recycle like a boss!

Project 1 – Coffee Table

Wood pallets are best used as starting material for coffee tables, center tables and side tables or night stands. They add an air of fancy interior to your home while being gentle on the pocket. Use them to center in a living room, entertain guests or as night stands in your personal space.

Materials

- Wooden Pallets
- Wood glue
- Hammer
- Wood polish
- Paint (optional)

Procedure

1. Start by taking the planks away from the pallet. This is not necessary if the planks are neatly joined as shown below. In this maintain the plain slab and get rid of any unnecessary wood.

2. Once you have a horizontal slab that will form the top of the coffee table, you can start working on the support system that will hold the top. Next, take single planks of the pallet to build a second tier of the table underneath the top. Using glue and nails for extra hold, glue wood together as shown in the image below. Use powerful wood glue and extra strength wood screws to secure at each of the four corners.

3. Next step is to use wood polish or protective spray to go all over your table top to ensure neatness and durability.

4. Your table top is now ready. Next, use wooden blocks to make the feet of the table according to your desire height. Another option is to use wheels that are available at hardware stores. This can make for a very creative potable coffee table.

5. That is what the finished product looks like. For some cool variations, you can add pops of color to your table according to the mood of your own room. The image shown below is an example.

Project 2 – Outdoor Garden/Patio furniture

When you think about garden furniture, the foremost thing that comes to mind is the durability of the product. Due to being placed in harsh conditions of the outside weather, garden furniture needs to be tough to take the battering. That is where wooden pallets come in. They are rough and tough and do not burn a hole through your pocket. You can customize them according to your own taste and needs.

Materials

- Wooden pallet
- Measuring tape
- Wood polish/ finish
- Wood glue
- Wood screws
- Upholstery to top the frame
- Paint protective spray

Procedure

1. When you get your pallet, they look something like the image shows. Cut them to your desired length according to your need. We will be using this to form the seating of the benches.

2. Use as many as you need to stack in order to reach your desired length. The image below shows 3 stacked on top of each other.

3. Use as many of these stacked pallets to make the bench seating depending on the size of your outdoor space. Arrange them as desired. The image shows an L-shaped arrangement of 15 pallets of 3s. You can vary your pattern pf arrangement depending upon the size and shape of space you are making the furniture for.

4. This is optional but if you need back to the benches, just use some single pallets and prop them upright against the wall. Where there is not a wall behind the bench, use nails to prop the back up.

5. Next is painting. This is also optional but it is in my opinion the best part of the job. That's because it gives it that polished and brand new look that we all rush to the furniture stores for. Any color can be used. Here, black was used. After you have finished painting it your favorite color, give it a coat of protective spray to avoid the harsh conditions of the outside weather.

Next step is to arrange some upholstery on top of the benches to make them homey and comfortable. You can buy colorful cushions from anywhere you like and arrange them as desired on top of the furniture. A table can also be made using the same arrangement of pallets as uses for making the seating of the benches as shown below.

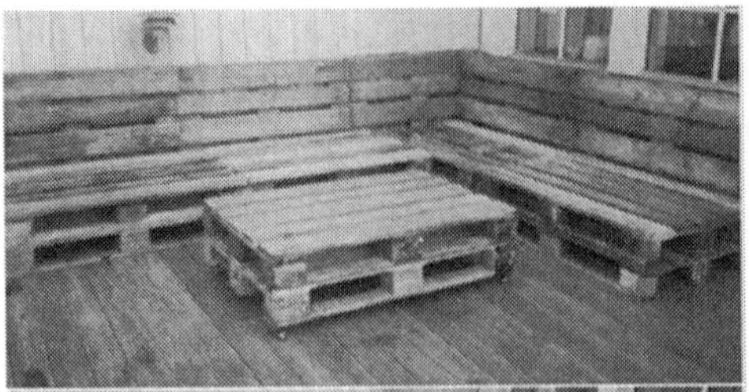
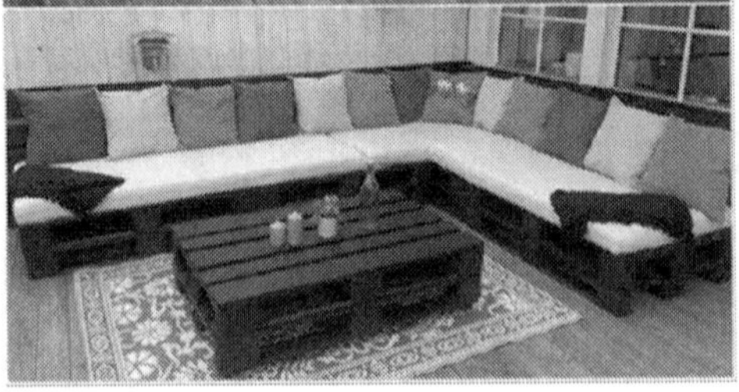

Chapter 3 – Wooden Pallet Art and Décor

These economical and pocket friendly wooden pallets have countless uses for the creative mind. We have already explores accessories and furniture. Now let's see what we can do with them for our art, décor and home improvement projects.

Project 1 – Wall cover up

This is an extremely simple and beginner friendly idea to use up and recycle wooden pallets. Also, it is a great way to cover up any horrible wall stains or ugly empty walls. A simple way to do that is to simply arrange the pallets side by side to cover up any wall. You can wood glue to securely fasten the pallets in palce. It is also possible to use any cutters and cut out shapes to decorate a wall in a children's bedroom as shown below.

t is also possible to paint the planks any bright colors or a combination of colors give your room an energetic and jolly look.

Project 2 – Wine Rack
This is a great idea to fill up that empty wall in the kitchen. It also beautifully stores all your gorgeous wine glassware and displays your wine collection.

1. Cut the planks in different sizes according to your desired lengths.

2. To make a three tier rectangular shelf as shown in the image above, three planks of varying sizes are required. One for the base, one for back and one for front. Cut them according to your preferred measurements.

3. Next, glue the planks together. Hammer a few iron nails in place for good support.

4. The slits of spaces in between the planks in the shelf will offer am automatic spot to hang up your wine glasses upside down.

http://stockpallets.com/wp-content/uploads/2015/11/DIY-Wooden-Pallet-Ideas-2.jpg

Project 3 – Ornamental Christmas tree

Materials

- Wooden Pallets
- Wood glue
- Hammer
- Wood polish
- Paint (optional)
- Ornaments and candles
- Measuring tape

Procedure

1. Start by taking the planks away from the pallet.
2. If the pallets are in need of a brush up, clean them away and take out old rusty nails.
3. Once you have the separated woken planks start cutting them up into descending lengths, going from shortest to longest. Make sure to mark the lengths using measuring tape before you start cutting because once the cut is made there is no wiggle room left to correct that.
4. Next, take two or three smaller planks and randomly place them horizontally across the width of the tree to make pace to keep candles and other decorative items.

5. Polish and paint as desired and this is what the finished product will look like.

Project 4 – Wooden Pallet Wall Art

Nobody likes empty white walls. In order to give a home feel to the house, wall hangings prove to be a very convenient option. But there is a small issue with good art. It is expensive! We walk into am art store looking for something to hang up n that horrid empty wall and we find ourselves fishing pockets for money which to be honest are better put to some other useful purpose.

DIY wall art projects have recently become a very popular and easy way to decorate your walls in a pocket friendly yet stylish manner. Here we will share a few simple examples that you can use to decorate your own walls yourself.

Materials

- Wooden pallet
- Measuring tape
- Wood polish/ finish
- Frame Hanger hooks
- White paper
- Spray paint in white

Procedure

1. First and foremost, take the pallet apart. This will result in individual planks of wood.
2. Secondly, print out a desired saying which you wish to display on your wall art.
3. Once you have your saying printed, it is time to make your own paper stencil. Following the letters on the paper, cut them out leaving letter shaped hollows as shown below.
4. Once you have that in order, arrange the planks of wood in the desired shape and glue them together in place using wood glue. Once that is done,

carefully place the stencil onto the planks and spray paint through the letters. Let dry and remove stencil.

5. Once this is all dry, screw the frame hangers at the back or simply use a string to hang the pallet to a hook on the wall. Your finished product should look like this.

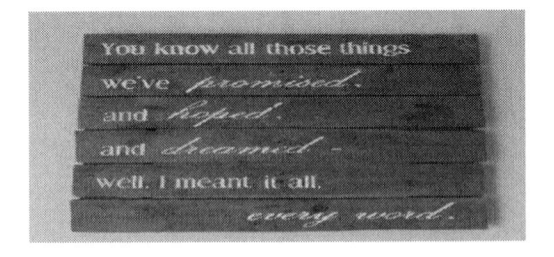

6. Alternatively, you can use your own art and paint over the wooden planks with creative ideas. Once sample is shown below.

Project 5 – Lamp base

When you take so many DIY wood pallet projects, you are bound to have some cutting of wood lying over here and there. Well fear not! Because we have a five star solution to that. This is also a great way to recycle that old lamp we all have lying around whose base we cannot tolerate anymore. A useful and stylish lamp base can be created as follows.

Procedure

1. Collect all the wooden blocks lying around of varying sizes. Make sure they are not too big or too small since they can be harder to work with. If they are too big, trim them to be around 5 to 6 inches each.

2. Using wood glue to glue the pieces together to form an irregular pyramid.

3. Using a drill machine, carefully drill a hole through the middle of the vertical pyramid. This will be used to pass the wire to light the lamp.

4. Next, using small screws secure the base of the lamp rod to the base of the pyramid.

5. Pass the electric cord down the middle hole that you earlier drilled.
6. Throw on a shade and you have got yourself a lamp. Paint and polish are optional to add color and energy.

Chapter 4 – DIY Garden Racks and Décor from Wood Pallets

The garden or an outdoor space serves as a haven when you get home on days that you are tired and are looking to unwind in the comfort of your own but you also need a boost of fresh air. A garden is an ideal option for lounging and spending some quality time with family as well as for entertaining friends and guests. A garden that is pleasing to the eyes as well as comfortable forms an integral part of your living space.

So evidently it makes sense to pay attention to the decor and organization of your home garden or outdoor space. In this chapter, we will discuss some ideas to help you work in a budget friendly manner to decorate your garden without upsetting your entire budget. We have out forth ideas and projects that can be followed exactly or can be customized to cater individual preferences and needs.

Project 1 – Pot Rack

This handy little table serves as a great way to arrange those little flowering potted plants that form an attractive and eye catching display.

Material

- 3 Wooden Pallets
- Wood glue
- Wood screws
- Hammer
- Wood polish
- Paint (optional)

- Potted plants

Procedure

1. For this project, we will be using one of the pallets as it is. This will form the top part of the rack which will be used to hold the potted plants. When you get your pallet it looks like it is shown in the image below. We will use it as it is.

2. Next, take the second pallet and break apart the planks to separate them. Be careful while taking out the old nails. We will use the individual planks to form side support of the rack. Make sure to nail the planks to the sides to ensure sturdy frame. You can also use wood glue for this purpose.

3. Next, take the third pallet and use it to form the base of the rack. This will look similar to the top and can be used to house garden tools and hardware.

4. If you wish, the pot rack can be painted a bright color or an elegant white. The finished product will look like this.

Project 2 – Vertical Herb Garden

Not all of us have the luxury to afford huge gardens. Most populace lives in apartment buildings. However economical, this comes at a price. It mean that you will not have a ground garden. But not to worry, this can be solved. Most apartment building s have a small balcony or an outdoor area that gets ample light and air and oxygen. What you can do is use simple DIY project ideas using wood pallets to make a vertical herb or kitchen garden and have access to fresh herbs while on a cooking spree. You can enjoy fresh herbs that you grow from scratch.

Material

- 1 full size Wooden Pallet
- Wood glue/ Brad nails
- Wood polish/ paint
- Paint (optional)

- Cardboard or plastic rectangular boxes for holding mud
- Mud or dirt for planting
- Herbs

Procedure

1. Take a full sized wood pallet and cut it into half so that the length of the racks and each shelf would stay the same.
2. Remove the plank that runs through the midst of the pallet so you will be able to use the outsides of the pallet for the outsides of your rack making it look even.
3. Use brad nails to screw the shelves in your desired arrangement.
4. Fix the mud holding boxes in each of the shelves
5. Make sure to drill a hole through each box for drainage and air circulation

6. Plant herbs and water regularly and you have your very own vertical herb garden.
7. If desired, the rack can be painted or used as it is.

Project 3 – Garden Path

Making your own garden wood pallet path is very easy. Not only that, it is also very budget friendly and an economical way to spice up your boring garden at a price exponentially cheaper than landscaping projects.

Material

- Wooden Pallet
- Wood polish/ paint
- Paint (optional)
- Mud

Procedure

1. For this project you will need to make sure you have available a muddy patch in your garden that does not have grass or any other plants growing on it. You will need clear sticky mud base to ensure holding of the palettes.

2. Next, take your wooden pallets and take them apart by taking out old nails that hold them together in place. Be careful while performing this step. You will now have individual wooden planks.

3. Now, dig your soft ground a little lower than the driveway. This makes sure that when the boards are placed, it is an even transition when you walk up from outside on to your wood path to your garden.

4. Now, simply place the wooden planks wither immediately adjacent to one another or with a little gap in between according to your personal preference. Although they will hold pretty well due to weight and size but for extra hold, make sure to press them into the dirt so it stays put.

5. Keep some weight on the planks and give them time to set.

6. This is a great way to enhance your garden area. And it is easy to reverse whenever you want to change into something else.

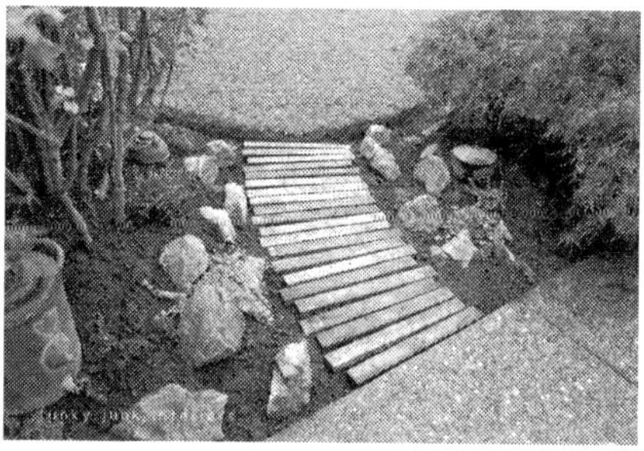

Conclusion

No home can exists without décor and furniture. And what better way to start out your own line for your own home using easy DIY projects. Wooden pallets are an extremely economical and budget friendly material to use as a base for home improvement and decor projects. It is not often that we have a huge budget for enhancing the interior and outdoor space of our living space but we seem to need change often. Moreover, home décor can be an excessively expensive task that does not help you if you are somebody on a budget. This is exactly why DIY projects like this one are very suitable options.

Wood pallets are readily available for recycling and do not cost a bunch which is what makes them a prime candidate for use. They are durable, customizable according to taste and needs and also give the home an esthetic look due to the wood texture.

After reading this book, you will now be able to take this as guidance to create your very own furniture yourself which is not only feasible from an economic point of view but also is a very satisfying experience. The book contains easy to follow guidelines and ideas regarding furniture making and art and décor projects that will help you every step of the way. You can make furniture for to decorate your own home, make them as house warming gifts for your friends and also for selling to customers. Not only is the experience satisfying but also ensues a sense of pride. If you are not as great in the beginning of your projects, do not panic. Just keep going, start with some beginner projects first and carefully follow guideline and precaution and you will see that practice makes a man perfect.

So what's the hold up? Grab the book and those wooden pallets and Ready, Set, Tools!

15 Wood Pallet Projects for Beginners

Introduction

We all want a home that's well-decorated, functional, and personal, but not everyone can spend a fortune ordering expensive pieces of furniture from catalogs, and some would like to create a home that's unique to their personality. There's no better way to do all that than to create your own furniture, decorations, and functional pieces in your home from wood pallets. Pallets are everywhere. They're a huge part of the shipping industry, but if you're worried about where your pallet may have been, you can always order a new one from a manufacturer.

If you're going to go with used pallets, then here are some things you want to keep an eye out for.

Number one, you want to make sure the pallet has a logo stamped on it. Not all pallets will have one because it could have been rubbed off during shipping, and stamping pallets is not always mandatory depending on which country it's coming from. These are the following codes for the treatment code:

- *MB: Methyl Bromide*
- *HT: Heat Treated*
- *KD: Kiln Dried*
- *DB: Debarked*

Heat treated pallets are made in the United States or Canada and undergo a pest control that's known as heat treating. This entails heating the pallet to a core temperature of one hundred and thirty-three degrees Fahrenheit for softwood to one hundred and forty degrees Fahrenheit for a hardwood pallet for thirty minutes. These are not harmful to a person's health and are safe if not treated with anything else.

Kiln dried wood is to reduce the moisture content of the wood. That means it will control fungal growth, warping, and other quality control features. These boards don't normally reach temperatures that the heat treated boards do, but it's enough to keep them safe.

Methyl bromide fumigation is a powerful pesticide that has been linked to ozone layer depletion and is harmful to human health. This is banned in Canada, but it's used in other countries and poses a health risk. Do not use this as firewood or in a craft project as it's harmful to your health!

Debarked boards are just as they sound. It means the wood was debarked using the IPPC regulations. This doesn't indicate the safety of a pallet, so be sure to check for the other codes mentioned.

With that being said, you can now begin your journey of creating awesome projects with pallets!

Chapter 1 - Wood Pallet Wall

If you want to add some zing to your bedroom wall or maybe you want to make a living room fireplace look rustic, break apart some wood pallets and start attaching them to your wall! It's actually pretty simple and makes your room look cozy and cottage-like.

Materials

- Safety Gloves
- Nail gun
- Pallets
- Nails
- Wood Glue
- Wood Stain

Note: The amount of pallets you'll need will depend on the size of your wall, as will the amount of nails you'll need. Be sure to measure the wall and estimate how much wood you'll need to complete the project before beginning. It's better to purchase more and have some left over for a smaller project rather than not having enough, so overestimate.

Directions

1. Take apart the pallets gently, attempting not to break apart the top and bottom pieces that you'll be using on the wall.
2. Prepare the wall through coating it with some primer or at least cleaning it. After the wall has been prepared, measure to see how many pallets you'll need.

3. Apply some wood glue to one side of the pallet piece and glue it to the wall, beginning at the top or lower right or left corner.

4. Use the nail gun in the four corners of the pallet to keep it in place. Repeat these first four steps until the entire wall has been covered.

5. If you have any gaps on the edges of the wall, measure that space and cut some pieces to fit so that you cover the entire wall.

6. If you want a rustic look, cover up the nails with some wood putty and wait twenty-four hours before staining the entire wall.

Chapter 2 - Wine Rack

This is a simple, one bottle wine rack that holds glasses, too.

Materials

- (2) 4.75"x43.5" Pallet Boards
- (2) 4.75"x4" Pallet Boards
- Black Paint
- Table Saw
- Sander
- Drill
- Clamps

Directions

1. Cut all the pieces of wood to size and sand them. Just sand to get off the dirt for now and worry about a finer sanding later.

2. Make a hole with a 38mm drill bit so that it will fit almost any bottle. Use the 25mm drill bit to make the large opening in the center of the bottom piece and then use a 15mm drill bit to make the opening to the larger hole so you can slide the glasses in.

3. Pre-drilling any holes makes the assembly a lot easier. In addition, you want to use some clamps to get it together properly. Use some wood glue to glue the four pieces together, making sure the bottom piece is on the bottom and facing out properly to slide in the glasses, and the opening for

the bottle is on the side you'd like it on. Then clamp them together and allow them to sit overnight to cure.

4. Before you paint, you need to sand off the entire piece now. Use 60 to 120, then 180 to 240 to get a smooth finish. You want to sand until there is a soft, silky feeling when you touch the wood.

5. You can use any type or color of paint you want on your wine rack. This tutorial uses black paint, but you can use another color or even stain the pieces to give it a cozier look.

6. Wait twenty-four hours after you finish he piece and then hang it on the wall with a few hooks and enjoy!

Chapter 3 - Planter

This planter is good for a small tree or a large tomato plant and can be used indoors or outdoors.

Materials

- 4 Pieces of Pallet Wood The Same Length (For the Legs)
- 8 Side Bars (Make Sure They're The Width of the Planter)
- Nails
- Nail Gun
- Side Panel Pieces

Directions

1. Cut the four legs the height you want your planter to be, and then cut the eight sidebars to the width you want your planter to be. Then disassemble the rest of the pallet if you haven't already and set aside planks for your sides.

2. Build two matching sides. The lower side piece shouldn't touch the ground so that you avoid water. You should end up with two legs with two sidebars in between for each side, one sidebar at the top and one at the bottom on the inside.

3. Then use the remaining side bars to attach your two sides together to make a cube.

4. Use nails for the sides as you attach them to the sidebars, one nail on the bottom and one on the top. You don't need a lot because they're not load bearing.

5. Once you're done, make a cube to put on the top as a frame to hide any shorter or longer pieces of siding.

6. Put an old bin or a bucket in the center that's low enough to be hidden by the planter and put a plant in it!

Chapter 4 - Decorative Tray

You won't need much to make this decorate tray, but it'll end up looking like something you bought from an expensive art gallery by the time you're finished!

Materials

- A Dismantled Pallet
- 1 ¾" Nails
- Wood Glue
- Dark Stain
- 2 Cabinet Door Hinges
- Gloves
- Petroleum Jelly
- Spray Paint
- Paper Towels
- Foam Brushes
- Screw Driver
- Drill Bit
- Sander

Directions

1. Disassemble your pallet and make sure you have three unbroken deck boards. Cut out two thirteen inches and four twenty-two inch deck boards.

Some dent or imperfections will add some character, but make sure the boards are not broken. Sand the rough edges and the top until you reach your desired smoothness.

2. Add a good amount of wood glue between the two thirteen inch boards on the edges where they will go together and add some to the four twenty-two inch boards. Secure them together and allow them to dry.

3. With a sponge brush, add a little stain with a random pattern. Once it's been absorbed, smear the petroleum jelly on the parts you want to stay visible.

4. Now spray paint your tray and allow it to dry completely. You might need a few coats to get it covered. Once it's dry, wipe it with some paper towel to get rid of the petroleum jelly and you'll see the dark stain showing through.

5. Now, add the hardware to complete the look. Use some cabinet door hardware and attach them on either side of the shorter ends of the tray so you can easily pick it up.

Chapter 5 - Electronics Shelf

Are you tired of your entertainment center not being able to hold all the electronic devices you have for your television? Does your child need something in their room to hold their equipment but you don't want to purchase an expensive entertainment center for them? Then make an electronics shelf!

Materials

- 1 Pallet
- Screws and Drill
- ½" Thick Scrap Piece of Wood
- Sander
- Shelves or Boards
- Shelf Brackets

Directions

1. Sand off any rough edges and dust off the cobwebs and dirt.
2. Choose the height you prefer your shelves to be and then screw the brackets onto the pallet. If the holes don't line up, then use some extra-long screws to reach the vertical two by fours.
3. You need to locate a stud to screw the pallet into on the wall. Due to trim at the bottom of your wall, use a small piece of scrap wood the same depth as your trim and put it between the pallet and the wall before you screw it into the stud. This keeps it standing straight.

4. Screw on the shelves. Weave the cords through the pallet for your electronics and plug them in!

Chapter 6 - Bike Rack

Bike racks can be expensive, but using two pallets and attaching them together makes an awesome bike rack you can paint or even just finish with some wood stain to make it look chic!

Materials

- 1 Pallet with Thinner Boards
- 1 Pallet with Larger Boards

Directions

1. The pallet with the thinner boards is the one you will be leaning against the wall because the narrower slots will hold the bike wheels. The other pallet is going to go upside down.

2. For the pallet that's sitting on the ground, you want a little more wiggle-room to line up the wheels to fit into the vertical slots. You can do this through setting the pallet with the boards down. This provides a little 'well' for the wheels and gives you a cross-brace to keep the wheel from rolling out of place. Note that you need a little distance from the wall and the bottom pallet so you can lean the top pallet against the wall to keep it steady.

3. Put your bikes on!

Chapter 7 - Herb Trough

You may have made the planter already, but herb troughs are a little different. This is more like a feed trough design so you can put many more herbs in the planter without having to use too much dirt.

Materials

- 2-3 Pallets
- Wood Screws
- Cordless Drill

Directions

1. Measure out the size you want your herb box to be. A good place to start would be three feet long by a foot wide. This will allow you to put in plenty of herb plants!

2. Now measure out a frame. You'll need four legs attached together by a three foot by one-foot frame. Then put another frame on the top.

3. Now attach your sides lengthwise. You can put a plastic liner on the inside of the box in order to keep the wood protected and make your box last longer.

4. Fill it up with dirt and plant your herbs!

Chapter 8 - Spice Rack

Are you tired of your small spice rack and you'd like something a little larger? Then make a spice rack out of a pallet!

Materials

- 1 Pallet
- Sander
- Wood Glue

Directions

1. First you want to dismantle and lay out the spice rack pattern with your pallet. To dismantle the pallet, stand it on its side and use a saw to cut through the nails on either end. This lets you use the entire length of the board without splitting the back or the board. When it's dismantled, lay out the boards that will work for your space where you want to put the rack. Cut the boards as little as possible if you have a large space. Know that some boards will be different widths and might need to be used in another project. Sand all the boards on all sides before you move on.

2. Now, use some wood glue to connect the four sides of the rack together. Due to not wanting to cut the boards too much, you'll need to use the full length of the pallet boards for the sides and only cut the ones that you will use lengthwise. Wood glue will keep everything together just fine as long as you clamp it and you let it sit overnight to cure.

3. When the back and the frame are together, insert the boards you'll be using for the shelves and glue them from the sides. The measurements for

the height of the shelves will be based on the different heights of spices, or you can put the shelves all in at an even distance.

4. Before you hang the rack, you might want to run the sander over it again just to get rid of any glue pieces or any little splintered pieces that might have come up throughout your process. If you don't know where the wood came from that you're using, you might want to spray it with a bleach solution to make it safe for the kitchen.

Chapter 9 - Compost Bin

Compost bins are excellent additions to any garden, whether it's a vegetable or flower garden. To create a really easy compost bin you can start adding kitchen scraps to right away, just grab yourself four pallets and get started with this tutorial!

Materials

- 4 Pallets
- 14 Gauge Wire
- Hinges
- Latch

Directions

1. Begin by cutting the wire to eighteen inch long pieces and strap the side and back pallets together through twisting the wire tight. Don't overdo it or the wire will snap. Two pieces of wire twisted one each corner should be fine.

2. Put a landscape pole on the hinge side of the bin. The pallets are not light so you need some support for the door pallet. Hammer the pole into the ground about a foot.

3. Add the hinges to the hinge side. Put a spacer on the bottom with some leftover landscaping pole and attach that with screws. This allows some ventilation for the compost because all the other sides are sitting on the ground.

4. Add a latch if you want to keep any children or animals out of your bin.

5. If you live in a dry climate, you need moisture in your bin to keep it composting. So add some plastic to the top to keep it moist and warm inside.

Chapter 10 - Desktop Planter

Does your desktop need a little green on it, but you don't want to spend too much green to get it? Then use some scrap pieces of pallet from your other projects to make yourself a little desktop planter!

Materials

- Pallet Pieces
- Plastic Cups
- Nails
- Wood Glue
- Potting Mix
- The Plant
- Hammer
- Saw

Directions

1. It's as easy as measuring out the wood and gluing it together. Let's use the example of a four inch by four-inch planter. Measure the width of the wood and subtract it from four inches. Sand the pieces and measure out the bottom.

2. Glue the wood together and nail on the bottom. Then use a little wood putty between the pieces if you want a more contemporary design, and sand it again.

3. You can then paint it any color you wish or leave it unfinished for a rustic look.

4. Put the plastic cup inside and put a plant in it!

Chapter 11 - See Thru Birdhouse

Have you ever wondered what it was like to look inside a bird house while the birds were actually using it? Well, now you can with this see-through birdhouse that features a screen at the back so you can hang it near a window in order to look inside!

Materials

- Saw
- Pallet planks
- Drill
- Hammer
- Hole saw kit
- Ruler
- Nails
- Pen

Directions

1. To make the window, you'll want to take the cover off an old CD case and bend the edges forward very carefully. There'll be a snap and then you'll have a clean break. Sand down the edges to make it smooth and get rid of any sharp edges. Then use a drill to make a small hole in every corner.

2. Use some pallet planks to make the birdhouse. The plank you'll want to use should be six inches wide and half an inch thick. Use a ruler to mark the wood at five, ten, fifteen, and twenty inches. This gives you four six by

five-inch pieces for the walls. Then measure and cut the front panel of the house so that it fits within the interior of the walls when it's put together. It should be four and a half inches squared.

3. For this birdhouse, we will be making the hole one and a half inches wide, which is best for small birds. Mark the center point of the two adjacent sides of the four and a half inch squared piece. Draw a line between these two points. Make a vertical line from corner to corner to make a cross. Measure one and a half inches down from your horizontal line to make a second line. Then make two more vertical lines three-quarters of an inch from the center vertical line.

You should now have a box. Figure out the center of the box by making an X from corner to corner. Now you have the center point of the bird house entrance. Use a drill and a one and a half inch hole saw to cut out your hole.

4. This step of the process is optional. If you want to add a perch to the nest box, then drill a hole under the entrance and put a small piece of dowel inside with some wood glue.

5. Assemble the walls around the entrance so that the birdhouse is six inches deep. Use nails to put the wood together, four to five for every side, in an overlapping pattern so that it fits around the entrance. Then secure the plastic window on the back.

6. Hang your birdhouse in front of a window and wait for the birds to make a nest!

Chapter 12 - Spoon Shelf

Spoon shelves can be used just about anywhere in the home, but they make a statement when your guests enter and hang their jackets on silver spoons in your foyer. If you haven't guessed already, a spoon shelf is actually a piece of wood with spoons underneath that have been cut and bent into the shape of a hook. Look for some fancy, old-fashioned spoons at your local thrift shop to give this project a pop!

Materials

- 2 Wide Pallet Boards
- 3 Spoons
- Miter Saw
- Sand Paper
- Sander
- Brad Nailer
- Screw Driver
- ½" Screws

Directions

1. First let's begin with the pallet. You're going to need two of the wider boards and one side board. Cut the first board to thirty-four inches. The second board is going to be at twenty-eight inches. Now let's cut the side piece. You want the shape of the side piece to be noticeable on the shelf so measure three inches from the curve and cut the end off. Then put the piece up against the board and mark how long it should be.

2. Then sand the ends of all the pieces to make them smooth but don't sand them too much because you want a rustic look! Make sure you sand the edges and get any splinters off. Then dry fit the pieces together to make sure the look is good. Do a three-inch overhang on either side.

3. Use the brad nailer for this next step. Nail the base first and turn the back upside down and use a table to line it all up. Nail it through the back of the board into the side piece. Four nails should be good. Then lay the shelf on its back and line up your top. Remember the three-inch overhang on the sides! Nail it to the top into the side piece and then into the back piece. You're almost finished!

4. Now you want to stain it. You don't have to be too careful with this. Just get it on there with a rag or an old paint brush. Once you have it all covered, wipe off any excess with a clean rag. While the stain is drying, you can begin with the spoons.

5. You want to use old spoons from a thrift store and not your good silverware! Begin by laying the spoons face down on a hard surface. Be careful about the surface because this will mark up a wood table. Start at the middle of the spoon and work out toward the end. If you pound in one spot too much, you'll have to turn it over and pound from the other side, which will seriously weaken the metal. You want the spoon completely flat and bent away from the handle.

6. Now bend the handle so the design is facing outside of the bend. That way you'll see it when you hang it! For most, you'll be able to bend them with your hands but find something round so it's a smooth bend.

7. Use a drill press to put two one eight inch holes in the spoons. It's pretty simple, just drill one on top and one on the bottom of the face of the spoon. After the holes have been drilled, be sure to remove any metal shards with a file.

8. Now just screw on the screws with a half inch stainless steel screw. First measure between the two side pieces to find the center. Then screw in a center spoon. Then measure four inches away from the center and put in another spoon. The same on the other side.

Chapter 13 - Wine Box

This wine box makes the perfect carrier for a holiday gift to the in-laws, or cousins, or aunt, or whomever! This is a simple, elegant box with beautiful décor on it that will blow your receiver's mind away.

Materials
- Pallet Wood Planks
- Saw
- Planer
- Sander
- Router Saw
- Wood Glue

Directions
1. Gather some thirty-nine inch by five and a half inch pallet boards. Plan your layout so that the cuts will get rid of any nail holes.
2. Cut the boards down to a rough length. You'll be cutting them down to finish size later on. Basically, cut off the ends and the center section where the nail holes are.
3. Now plane down to a quarter inch thickness with the planer.
4. Take all four side pieces and rip them to five and a half inches and the top and bottom to five inches.
5. The long side boards should be cut to sixteen inches and the short sides should be cut to four and a half inches.

6. This is where things get a little fancy. You're going to need a quarter inch straight cut bit on the router table to a depth of a quarter of an inch. Bo the short end sides will get a quarter inch dado that will be a quarter of an inch from the edge. The longer sides will get a stopped dado on the bottom and a dado that ends on one side and through on the other side to all for the top to slide in and out.

7. Take one of the shorter pieces and cut off a quarter inch strip above your dado and save it. This will be glued to the top to act as a handle yet still keep the original lines of your box.

8. Now it's time to build your fancy wine box! Be sure to apply enough wood glue to every joint. Use some brad nails to help hold the box together until the glue dries. Even though it has butt joints, the box will be strong enough.

9. Now slide the top panel into the dado in the box and mark where you need to cut it. Then take the top panel and use the miter saw to chop off one end. Take the small piece that cut off the shorter side panel and glue that on like a little pull.

10. Now do some light sanding. You don't want to take the wood down too far or you'll get rid of that rustic look of the pallet boards. Sand the edges to get rid of any little splinters and slide the top panel on and sand the end so it's flush while it's in the closed position.

11. Now you can decorate the box with anything you want! If you're talented, you can paint the top, or you can use a photo transfer from an inkjet printer and apply a little lacquer to it.

Chapter 14 - Bat Box

Bats are actually very beneficial little critters to the environment, and if you have a problem in the attic, you can easily move them outside with one of these neat little projects! Just find a sunny area on the south side of your home and be sure to close off any areas that lead back into your home.

Materials

- Untreated Pallets
- Pry Bar
- Hammer
- Screws
- Drill
- Caulk
- Wood Stain
- Varnish
- Shingles
- Stapler

Directions

1. Be sure you're using a pallet that hasn't been chemically treated. Look for HT on it to make sure its heat treated because you don't want the bats becoming intoxicated.

2. Dismantling your pallet might be more of a challenge than you think. Not all of them are created equal, and some of them can be made for extremely heavy hauls. You'll most likely have to end up cutting off the ends of the planks because they'll be damaged by using the crowbar on them. That's okay. Just take your time and find spots you can pry on.

3. You'll want to plan out the box according to where you're located. You'll want to look up bats in your location and what they prefer. This tutorial is going to be for the Little Brown Bat since they're common. This is also a box for a colder climate as the bats will need less ventilation in order to stay warm. Cut the planks to twenty inches by twenty-four-inch lengths, with the center planks being nineteen and a quarter inch in length.

4. Bats have very strong feet and claws, but they will still need a little roughness to get a grip on their landing strip. Secure your plank with some clamps and make a score on the wood every half inch or so with a circular saw blade adjusted to an eighth-inch thickness. The planks will be uneven, so just adjust the blade a little lower for warps in the wood. Score the parts that will be interior surfaces and score the center planks on both sides.

5. Use a small diameter bit to predrill any nail holes so you don't split all the wood you just prepared.

6. Now for the assembling. Clamp down your center planks with the grooves on both sides facing each other. Then nail down the side piece and leave a quarter inch gap at the top to share heat across the center barrier. Turn it around and nail the other side piece, and be sure to check to make sure the angled roof cuts are on the same end. Then nail the roof on the top and be sure it's flush with the back planks. Now nail on the front and back planks.

7. Caulk any cracks and holes if you live in a colder climate. If you live in a warm climate, then be sure *not* to caulk cracks and holes because the bats need more ventilation. Wait for the caulk to dry before you paint or stain the exterior part of the box. For a colder climate, use a dark stain to absorb

more heat from the sunlight. Be sure the paint is water based, and then varnish the wood after the stain has dried.

8. When you install your bat box, you want to be near a known bat nesting area. The box needs to be at least twenty feet off the ground or as high as a ladder will take you. It should be about a thousand feet from any known open water sources. You need a wide area around the box that's not obstructed, and if you live in the north, the box should be in full sunlight to get as much heat as possible in the winter.

Chapter 15 - Raised Bed Garden

You've already seen a tutorial for a herb box, but this is a much larger raised bed garden that you can put pepper, tomato, eggplant, and so many other larger vegetables into! If you want to get fancy, you can even attach a trellis to the side for your climbing plants.

Materials

- Pallets
- Crow Bar
- Circular Saw
- Sander
- Nail Gun
- Nails
- Trim

Directions

1. You'll want to look for pallets that are free or low-cost because you'll need a few of them to complete this project. If you're near a warehouse business, just stop in and ask them if you can take a few pallets. Chances are they'll be ecstatic to get rid of them. Just make sure they're heat treated and not chemically treated if you're growing any vegetables you'll be consuming. The newer pallets are usually heat treated, but some of the older ones were treated with chemicals and should be avoided.

2. Once you have the pallets home, you'll want to tear them apart into usable pieces. This is harder than it sounds. You'll want a crowbar or pry bar to

gently each the boards apart. Or you can use a saws-all in order to get them apart by cutting the nails. That's the easiest way. Once the boards are off, you should have some notched out two by fours.

3. Now you need to cut your planks for the raised bed. It's best to use a circular saw for this process. Cut the wood into three or four-inch strips. Cut the boards down to thirty-six-inch pieces. You'll end up with three and four-inch boards that are thirty-six inches long.

4. Now you need to cut six fourteen inch pieces from the two by fours that came from the pallets. These are going to be the four corners of your raised bed and for the center of the boxes.

5. Now you need to group the planks together and lay them out. The raised bed will be a foot tall so you'll need to get a few three or four-inch pieces to make twelve inches. The sides will consist of four side sections and the two ends, so you'll need six groups of boards that will get you to twelve inches tall. You'll then lay out your six fourteen inch pieces of two by four to connect the corners and the centers of the long sides.

6. Once everything has been laid out, you'll then begin joining your side boards to the supports. Every side section is going to overlap the center of the support halfway and be secured with nails. The support will extend below the bottom and the corners. This gives it a little stability because you'll be putting it into the ground a bit. Use two nails per board and be sure to predrill the holes to avoid splitting the wood.

7. You'll then add a little trim around the top to make it look nice, or you can leave it plain to make it look rustic. Use some small nails to attach the trim.

8. Fill it up with dirt and start planting!

Conclusion

Always remember to look for a stamp and look for HT or KD to make sure your pallet is safe. Also, be aware that colored pallets are most likely used to transport chemicals and should be avoided, especially blue and red as these were used to transport harmful chemicals. If there is any questionability about where your pallet has come from, then don't use it in your home or for garden boxes! Harmful chemicals can leach out of the wood and be sucked into plants, which you then consume.

That being said, pallets are great materials for home projects and they are very safe as long as you follow the guidelines. They're also an inexpensive way to dress up your home just the way you like it!

I hope you enjoyed this eBook on pallet projects. If you did, please leave a review at your online eBook retailer's website.

Thank you for reading!

FREE Bonus Reminder

If you have not grabbed it yet, please go ahead and download your special bonus report *"DIY Projects. 13 Useful & Easy To Make DIY Projects To Save Money & Improve Your Home!"*

Simply Click the Button Below

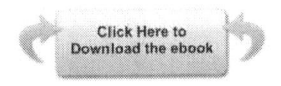

OR **Go to This Page**

http://diyhomecraft.com/free

BONUS #2: More Free Books

Do you want to receive more Free Books?

We have a mailing list where we send out our new Books when they go free on Kindle. Click on the link below to sign up for Free Book Promotions.

=> Sign Up for Free Book Promotions <=

OR Go to this URL

http://bit.ly/1WBb1Ek

Printed in Great Britain
by Amazon